MW00609149

Looking Back on 50 Years

as an

Old-School

Democrat

ALSO BY J. "RAY" SPARROW

Comments and Conversations:
On the Growth of Cary, North Carolina
1955-2015

Looking Back on 50 Years

as an

Old-School

Democrat

★ ★ ★ ★ ★

J. "RAY" SPARROW

Quotes on pages 5 and 6 are from ENCYCLOPEDIA OF NORTH CAROLINA edited by William S. Powell. Copyright © 2006 by the University of North Carolina Press. Used by permission of the publisher. www.uncpress.org.

Quotes on pages 12 and 23 are from THE PARADOX OF TAR HEEL POLITICS: THE PERSONALITIES, ELECTIONS, AND EVENTS THAT SHAPED MODERN NORTH CAROLINA by Rob Christensen. Copyright © 2010 by the University of North Carolina Press. Used by permission of the publisher. www.uncpress.org

Illustrations on back cover and pages 11, 20, 21, 59, and 74 by Jerry Miller. Despite reasonable attempts, the author was unable to locate copyright holders of the cartoons on pages 73 and 103.

COPYRIGHT © 2017
J. Ray Sparrow

All rights reserved. No part of this book may be used, reproduced or transmitted in any form or by any means, electronic or mechanical, including photograph, recording, or any information storage or retrieval system, without the express written permission of the author, except where permitted by law.

ISBN 978-1-59715-170-2

First Printing
Printed in the United States of America

FOR MELBA

Melba Sparrow

"What we have once enjoyed and deeply loved, we can never lose, for all we love deeply becomes a part of us."

HELEN KELLER

This book is dedicated to my wife, Melba Truelove Sparrow, who passed away after a long, courageous battle with cancer on June 18, 2016. She was not only my wife, she was my lover, and most of all, my friend. Our pastor, Carl Frasier, at First United Methodist Church of Cary, said it best in her eulogy:

> There are people that leave an imprint. They come into our lives and our lives are not the same. We are better, stronger, richer for

their having come our way. They leave an indelible mark on us. Melba Sparrow was one of those people.

Melba left an indelible mark on her family. She and Ray shared forty-three years of marriage, which included a business partnership as they worked together at Sparrow Construction Company. There was no question for any of them that it was she who handled the details of life. As recently as the week before her death, she sent Ray home from the hospital with a "to do" list. But it was more than a business partnership and "to do" lists for Ray and the family. It was a presence, an example she set.

Melba left an indelible mark on her friends. I suspect there are very few of you who never received a card from her—a hand-written card. Who does that anymore? Who takes the time to sit down and write just the correct word to someone who is sick? Struggling? Down? Melba did. She would buy and mail the cards by the hundreds.

Melba Sparrow left her imprint on this community. Cary is better—we are better—we are better because of Melba. From dozens of boards to numerous awards, there are few places in our common life that Melba did not touch. She was an encouragement to her pastor. In a short time, she left her mark here on our church. And she made a good Methodist, blending in her life that personal holiness of a life of prayer with social holiness, a life of good works to others. The Wake Hospital, Wake, Tech, the YMCA, Meredith College, the Chamber of Commerce—Melba influenced them all. As a twelve-year member of the town council and mayor pro tem, she shaped the Cary that we know now. She was a member of a generation of pioneering women who led and influenced beyond the home; she led and influenced the entire community. She left her imprint on Cary.

Contents

Foreword

J. "Ray" Sparrow is a retired licensed general contractor and Realtor, having built many houses, churches, and commercial buildings in and around Cary and the state of North Carolina. Ray is a retired major in the North Carolina National Guard, and served as the late governor Bob Scott's military aide. He has distinguished himself in the building trade many times over, serving as president of the North Carolina Home Builders' Association and as an inductee into the North Carolina Home Builders Hall of Fame. Ray served two terms as a legislator in the North Carolina House of Representatives and was presented the North Carolina Order of the Long Leaf Pine by Governor Jim Hunt in 1987. Among his many other distinctions, he is a past president of the Cary Chamber of Commerce, served eight years on the RDU Airport Authority, and is on the Board of Trustees of the Triangle YMCA.

It has been my good fortune to know Ray Sparrow for a little over sixty years. I first met him when he served as my National Guard company commander. Together we became active in the Jaycees at the local, state, and national levels, as well as in the Democratic Party working for county, state, and congressional candidates. Growing up in Durham as a good student-athlete who worked his way through high school and college, Ray became associated with the best people in the building industry, learned every skill they offered, and managed their biggest projects with compassion. In his work with the Chamber of Commerce, the Home Builders Association, and the Jaycees, he provided the leadership and knowledge needed to carry projects to new heights. In politics, Ray has done every volunteer job—from putting up signs, going door to door, and enlisting volunteers—to raising monies to help friends who were willing to serve as candidates.

You will read many letters here from elected officials and other friends who solicited Ray's help in improving or passing legislation in the North

Tom Bradshaw

Carolina General Assembly. You will also read some of the many letters he received from governors and other grateful candidates from both political parties thanking Ray for his input, for his knowledge, and for his help with the problems and challenges they faced in leading North Carolina. Many credited their successful campaigns to Ray Sparrow.

In his two terms in the North Carolina legislature, Ray Sparrow introduced and had passed over twenty bills. They say that was a record. The Raleigh *News & Observer* often praised Ray's work in the legislature, and just as often criticized him because he wasn't as liberal as they would have liked him to be. It is not surprising to me to know that Ray's favorite movie star growing up was John Wayne. Like the old cowboy, Ray always tried to do the right things for the right reasons. There is no finer public servant than Ray Sparrow. No matter what party you are affiliated with, I think you will enjoy this book!

Tom Bradshaw
Former mayor of Raleigh, North Carolina

Salute Ray Sparrow

As the lone Democrat voting for the gubernatorial veto last week, Rep. Ray Sparrow became about as popular in the legislature's marble courts as the fellow who pointed out the emperor's nudity.

But the party ranks that Sparrow broke are ranks that never should have been drawn against giving North Carolina governors the veto power.

Everyone knows that with an 82-38 majority the Democrats have the House under firm control— firm enough to override a veto, as a matter of fact. Why do they demean themselves falling into childish tantrums of partisanship like the one over the veto?

Because they did, Sparrow's lone dissent required real courage. Every other House Democrat, even those like Wake's Peggy Stamey who say they might support the veto for Democratic governors, were cowed into going along to defeat a Republican committee minority attempt to resurrect the veto question.

The partisan hyperbole and utter nonsense some leaders dished out against the measure should shame responsible Democrats. To hear Billy Watkins rant about how the GOP devil is "asking you to make the governor a member of the General Assembly,...to come over and vote with you," you'd think the veto was a wild-eyed revolutionary innovation in government, not a standard fixture in 49 states and the U.S. Constitution.

Up against such intimidating rhetoric, other Democrats had hinted Sparrow would be wise to take a walk instead of going on record as the lone bolter.

To his credit, this vigorous veteran of many a Democratic campaign stood firm. He adequately explained that "I'm just trying to change the Democratic Party so it will be more acceptable to the people,"—of whom two out of three tell pollsters they want a chance to vote on the veto.

Since he has favored the veto since before Jim Hunt became governor, what it came down to in the end was simple for Ray Sparrow: "Your first obligation is to vote your conscience." It's unfortunate that other members of the Wake delegation didn't have that same kind of courage and conviction.

State of North Carolina

James B. Hunt, Jr.
Governor

Reposing special confidence in the integrity, learning and zeal of

Ray Sparrow, Jr.

I do by these presents confer

The Order of the Long Leaf Pine

With the rank of Ambassador Extraordinary privileged
to enjoy fully all rights granted to members of this exalted order, among which
is the special privilege to propose the following North Carolina
Toast in select company anywhere in the free world:

Here's to the land
of the long leaf pine,
The summer land
where the sun doth shine,
Where the weak grow strong
and the strong grow great,
Here's to "down home,"
the Old North State!

By the Governor

Date: January 1·1985

I have spent nearly three-fourths of my life as a North Carolina Democrat, a little over fifty years. I was lucky to have a wife and a business partner who supported me during this period; my wife, Melba, and my business partner, Bill Jones, ran Sparrow Construction Company, allowing me to serve as a party organizer and a North Carolina legislator. In this small book I intend to give you some insight into what the Democratic Party was like between 1951 and 2001 when I was involved, and a little bit of what I think it is like today. Hopefully, you will enjoy my comments and gain some insight into why many people like me are no longer Democrats or Republicans.

You may also find of interest that I helped a few Republicans between 2002 and 2016, the year Donald Trump was elected president of the United States. That same year I changed my party registration to "unaffiliated" because I found that both parties had become so polarized that they weren't getting anything done. In my opinion, our political system is broken and it doesn't appear that it's going to be fixed anytime soon. I think one of the biggest problems is that when a candidate gets elected, the only consideration thereafter is reelection. Folks, we live in a time of spin and deception. In the old-school days, legislators would vote for a bill if it was a good bill, even if it was the opposite of his party's bill. Today, they won't vote for an opposite party's bill under any circumstances—good, bad, or indifferent!

Ray Sparrow

When I first started writing this book I included a lot of true stories about political sex affairs, political payoffs, sacks of money with no names attached, bid-rigging, and many other unethical acts that were going on in both the Democratic and Republican parties. After a great deal of consideration and advice from others, I decided that even though many of the people involved have passed away, it was not worth the hurt those disclosures might cause their families.

As you read about my experiences, please keep in mind that I have no regrets about my past involvement in the Democratic Party. For most of that time, I had many friends on both sides of the aisle, and I feel good about the legislation that I got passed. My experiences and comments are based on my own memories, admittedly a dangerous thing at my age. But perhaps you will learn something from my experiences, if you share my great concern about the future of our country and the state of North Carolina.

Two final advisories: Please note that some of the names in this book have been changed for obvious reasons. Also, "Politicians who tell the truth are seldom heard from again."

Enjoy!

Chapter One

Brief History of My Work as a Democrat

I GRADUATED FROM DURHAM HIGH SCHOOL in 1951 and got a job at Wright's Machinery in Durham shortly after graduation. Wright's Machinery was a twenty-year-old company that made machines that would wrap Cracker Barrel candy. The company was unionized a couple of months before I went to work for them. After a few weeks of working there, one of the union bosses came by and told me that if I wanted to continue working there, I would have to join the union. I'd begun to notice that the workers making the machines would sit down after lunch, stopping their work, and read or sleep the rest of the day. Well, I went to a couple of union meetings and wasn't impressed with what they had to offer, so I didn't sign up. About a week later, the union boss came by and said that if I didn't join the union, I would be blackballed and that nobody would speak to me. He also indicated that some "other things" might happen to me, too.

One day, I asked one of the workers why they stopped working in the middle of the day. He looked at me as if he thought I was crazy and said that under the union contract they could only make so many parts a day, and they could do that in a half a day. At the time, the head of the local AFL-CIO was Wilbur Hobby, whom I knew because his son was on our football team at Durham High. I quit the job after a couple of months and took a job with a friend who worked with a construction company in Durham. I started as a carpenters' helper and went to carpenter's school at night. Later, I became the general superintendent of the construction company. About two years after I quit the job at Wright's Machinery, the twenty-year-old company went bankrupt and closed down. Incidentally, Mr. Hobby later went to jail for misusing $1 million in job training money that the Hunt administration had funneled to two companies that Hobby controlled.

I worked for the Democratic Party for a little over fifty years. Actually, there were few Republicans in North Carolina during this time. A friend of mine asked me to help him with the Adlai Stevenson campaign in 1951-52. That was my first campaign, and I felt like I was doing something good, knocking on doors and passing out literature. Unfortunately, Stevenson lost. The next campaign I worked on was that of Harold D. Cooley in 1964, when Jim Gardner from Rocky Mount ran against him. Mr. Cooley had been in the US House of Representatives for about twenty years at a time in the early 1950s when the farmers in North Carolina had some political power. During the campaign I did a little driving for Mr. Cooley when he was in Raleigh. His sister had a house across from North Carolina State College, as it was known at the time, and he stayed there when he was in town. Mr. Cooley had been chairman of the US Department of Agriculture for many years. He was getting a little older and had a little problem with the bottle. Anyway, during the campaign, he and Jim Gardner were having a debate at the student union at NC State. After the debate, we went to his sister's house for a reception, and everybody there was telling him how great he did. I said I must've gone to the wrong debate because I thought that Jim won the debate. Mr. Cooley didn't like that one bit and I lost my job as driver, but Jim Gardner beat the devil out of Mr. Cooley and was elected to the US House of Representatives. Gardner not only won the Cooley race, he also served two terms as lieutenant governor under Governor Jim Martin.

Incidentally, from around 1960 until around 1990 while I was working in state politics in my spare time, I was also involved in the Raleigh City Council races and the Wake County commissioner and the Cary Town Council elections. In the Raleigh and Wake County elections we had about fifty businessmen businesspeople who would meet several times before the elections to decide who we would like to see run. Once decided, we would all work for the same candidates. Most of us belonged to the Raleigh Chamber of Commerce. From the city of Raleigh, we endorsed Avery Upchurch, Giles Coggins, Smedes York, Clarence Lightner, Tom Bradshaw, and Seby Jones. The county commissioners we endorsed were Stewart Adcock, Elizabeth Cofield, Mernie Hedrick, Betty Ann Knudsen, John Massey Jr., Jackson Nichols, Herbert Stout, Larry Zieverink, Edmund Aycock, R.B. Heater, Vernon Malone, Charles Montgomery, Gary Pendleton, and Betty Lou Ward. In Cary, we supported as mayors for the Cary Town Council Waldo Rood, Dr. E.B. Davis, Joe Versey, Fred Bond, Harold Ridder, Koka Booth, Ernie McAllister, and Harold Weinbrecht Jr. If you are from the area, you will recognize most of the names as some of the outstanding leaders in Raleigh and Cary. I might add that almost all of them were Democrats, and I either worked their campaigns or supported them.

Later on, in 1960, I worked in the Terry Sanford campaign. I knew Terry because he and I were in the National Guard together. In 1964 I also worked on the Lyndon Johnson campaign for US president, and the Dan K. Moore campaign for North Carolina governor in 1965. Then, in 1972 I became Nick Galifianakis's Wake County campaign manager. Nick was already in the US House and was running against Jesse Helms. He was also from Durham, and I knew his family because I played football with his brother, Harry, on the 1951 Durham High School football team (we won the state championship that year). Interestingly, one of Nick's family members, Zach Galifianakis, is a movie star, and as I write this, he is making a movie here in North Carolina about the demise of the Democratic Party. Another campaign I worked with several times was for Congressman Ike Andrews. Since I was very involved with the

IKE ANDREWS
4TH DISTRICT, NORTH CAROLINA

COMMITTEE:
EDUCATION AND LABOR

Congress of the United States
House of Representatives
Washington, D.C. 20515

May 18, 1982

Mr. Ray Sparrow
1119 Queensferry Road
Cary, NC 27511

Dear Ray:

You continue to amaze me --- and you are an
inspiration.

You seem to be able to do virtually everything
and in a manner as organized as to always be at
leisure and have ample time for every person and
cause --- even the painting of a neighbors door.

I am truly grateful.

Sincerely yours,

Ike Andrews
Member of Congress

IA:KCH

North Carolina Home Builders Association, I met often with Ike in Washington, DC. He represented our district and had an office in Cary.

Before I go on about my experiences in the Democratic Party in this period from about 1951 to 2016, I want to give you a little history and insight into how the Democratic Party came into being in North Carolina. The excerpts below are taken from *The Encyclopedia of North Carolina*, edited by William S. Powell and published by the University of North Carolina Press in 2006.

> The Democratic Party has wielded great political power in N.C. The state's politics have largely been defined by periods of unchallenged, one-party Democratic rule interrupted by other successful movements that have competed against and helped shape Democratic policies. Democrats trace their roots to the Democratic-Republican Party, or Jeffersonian Republican Party of the early 1790s. Jeffersonian Republicans believed in a strict interpretation of the U.S. Constitution and the advancement of state rights over a powerful national government. (p. 334)

> After the Civil War, the Southern Democratic wing (sometimes called the Conservative Party) became the primary political alternative to Republican Reconstruction policies. In North Carolina, Democratic leaders branded Republicans as callous outsiders who represented Northern and "black" interests at the expense of the natural-born white population. The Ku Klux Klan served as an unofficial but effective tool of political terrorism for these conservative Democrats, often preventing Republicans of both races from voting. By 1876, when Zebulon B. Vance was reelected governor more than a decade after his previous term had ended, the Conservatives had clearly emerged as the state's dominant political force and reclaimed leadership of the Democratic Party.

The success of the Populist Party among small farmers led to a Populist-Republican "Fusion" that was able to win control of both houses of the legislature in 1894 and elect a Republican governor in 1896. However, intense Democrat campaigning based on a doctrine of white supremacy succeeded in returning Democrats to power in 1898. One of their first actions back in office was to amend the state constitution to effectively disenfranchise black voters through a poll tax, literacy test, and grandfather clause. Disenfranchisement gave Democrats firm control of state politics, a one-party domination not seriously challenged until the 1960s and 1970s. (p. 335)

By the end of the twentieth century, the state's one-party political system, which had been so influential in shaping North Carolina's history since the Civil War, had vanished. The Republican Party had significantly boosted its numbers by absorbing the traditionalism abandoned by the Democrat Party's progressive wing, leaving state Democrats struggling to redefine themselves in this new ideological climate. Most Democrats refashioned themselves as moderates, adopting liberal positions on social issues such as racial equality and women's rights to appease the party's new base while continuing their traditional promotion of the state's economic development, even as businesses increasingly turned to the Republican Party. This balancing act proved crucial to the Democrats' survival, for although it seemed that N.C. preferred Republicans as their US Representatives, and Presidents, in 2005 Democrats still outnumbered Republicans in the General Assembly and occupied most of their top state offices, including the governorships. (pp. 335–37)

North Carolina
Department of Transportation
P.O. Box 25201   Raleigh 27611   (919) 733-2520

James B. Hunt, Jr., Governor

Thomas W. Bradshaw, Jr., Secretary

May 22, 1980

Ms. Christine Bunn
Executive Officer
Raleigh-Wake Homebuilders Association
1301 Annapolis Drive
Raleigh, North Carolina

RE: Ray Sparrow

Dear Ms. Bunn:

I am extremely proud to support the nomination of Ray Sparrow as the Homebuilder of the Year for North Carolina. I have known Ray for more than 20 years, long before he decided to enter the building business. It is my personal feeling when Ray decided to join the profession he set his goal to be the very best. In the years of service he has given, I know of no one who has worked harder to raise the level of professionalism of the industry within the state.

Ray's early contributions include helping organize the many committees in his local and state association. He has always sought ways to broaden the career opportunities in the business. His many accomplishments are reflected in an improved Parade of Homes program, public affairs seminars, legislative initiatives, and improved regulations governing all home builders in North Carolina.

During Ray's tenure as a director, officer, and president of the Raleigh-Wake Homebuilders Association, our organization grew and prospered as a result of his dynamic leadership. He contributed a sense of meaning and purpose in setting goals and objectives for our organization that led to the establishment of high standards and improved creditability with the public.

In recognition of Ray's many contributions, many chapters throughout North Carolina encouraged him to seek the office of state president. He conducted himself in that office in the same manner as when he served his local chapter. During his term as president, the growth in membership was unprecedented. He was instrumental in developing new chapters and encouraging professional activities in all of the local chapters.

As a professional builder he has earned the reputation as a craftsman, knowledgeable of his product and known for high quality of workmanship. I am proud to join his many friends and associates in supporting his nomination for Builder of the Year. It is an honor well deserved.

Sincerely yours,

Thomas W. Bradshaw, Jr.
Secretary

Chapter Two

Governors Scott and Hunt Campaigns

IN 1968 I GOT VERY INVOLVED in the Bob Scott for governor campaign through a friend of mine named Chuck Barber. I knew Chuck through the National Guard, and we both served as military aides to Governor Scott while he was in office. Chuck was at one time the chairman of the Democratic Party in North Carolina. He lived in Durham, and while he was chairman, someone put a bomb in his mailbox. Luckily, no one was hurt when the bomb exploded. When Bob Scott was elected governor, he asked me to be state campaign manager for Edmund Muskie for US

president in the 1972 campaign. Muskie was in the lead at that time, and Governor Scott thought that Muskie was going to be our next president. I think Scott thought that Muskie, like John Kennedy, whom Governor Terry Sanford helped, could do a lot for Scott when he got to be president.

Bob Scott pinning on the Military Aide medal

We first opened a two-room office in the Sir Walter Hotel in

FOR IMMEDIATE RELEASE

Governor Bob Scott, Chairman of the North Carolina Citizens for Muskie Committee, announced today the appointment of Julian Raymond Sparrow as State Campaign Coordinator for the Muskie for President Campaign in North Carolina.

Sparrow, a 38-years-old Raleigh contractor, will coordinate campaign activities from the State headquarters, which is located in the Sir Walter Hotel.

Mrs. Ruth Reynolds, of Raleigh, who worked in the 1971 General Assembly and more recently as a staff member of the State Democratic Executive Committee, will serve as the State headquarters office manager.

The State campaign office for Muskie for President will be open full time, beginning Monday, February 21. It is located in Room 101 in the Sir Walter Hotel.

Sparrow is the son of Mr. and Mrs. Julian Franklin Sparrow, of Durham. He graduated from Durham High School in 1951 and then attended the School of Design at North Carolina State University. He was employed by Leif Valand and Associates, Architects, of Raleigh, for ten years and now is President of Ray Sparrow Construction Company, of Raleigh, dealing in both commercial and residential building.

He is a Major in the North Carolina National Guard, a Baptist, former President of the Cary Jaycees, Vice President and Administrative National Director of the North Carolina Jaycees, and President of North Carolina Jaycees International Senate membership.

He has served on the Cary Planning and Zoning Board and the Board of Directors of Cary Rural Fire Department.

Sparrow has been an active Democrat in Wake County--serving on Cary precinct committees and was 1968 Wake Coordinator for Young Voters for Bob Scott.

2/16/72

Raleigh. At that time the Sir Walter Hotel was the hangout for all state politicians. We later moved to a larger area next to my construction office on West Johnson Street. The Scott people furnished desks, typewriters, and office equipment. They also furnished six to eight ladies to type letters to voters. Later I found out that these ladies were full-time employees of the Department of Motor

Sir Walter Hotel, Raleigh, NC

Vehicles. During this time I met our now-congressman David Price for the first time while flying with Governor Scott to Washington, DC. We were on the state plane, the *Cardinal*, on our way to meet with Ed Muskie and some of his team. David Price was their state coordinator. Even though David was very liberal, I really liked him.

I remember Muskie calling to ask if I would go to the Democratic Convention, which was held in Miami, Florida. He thought that the convention might be deadlocked and that they still might choose him. At that time, I was very involved in the Home Builders' Association and had already committed to a Home Builders Convention. Muskie didn't win the Democratic nomination; Hubert Humphrey did. But then Richard Nixon beat Humphrey.

Incidentally, one day while I was working in the campaign, a fellow Democratic named Zeno Ponder came into my office and introduced himself and said he wanted to pick up some information on the Muskie campaign. If you don't know who Zeno Ponder is, then you have never been to Madison County, North Carolina, which borders on Tennessee. In

The Paradox of Tar Heel Politics: The Personalities, Elections, and Events that Shaped Modern North Carolina, Rob Christensen wrote that Zeno and his brother E. V. Ponder ruled Madison County for many years, running "the most famous courthouse machine in the state from the 1950s through the 1980s. Politics was rough in Madison County. Men sometimes carried guns to voting places. Zeno Ponder's house was once dynamited, and there was no end to the jokes about 'graveyard voting.'" One I remember was about a friend of his from the State Elections Board calling him the night of a state election asking where his vote totals were for the county elections. The board official told him that all the other votes were in. As the story goes, Zeno told him that they hadn't "finished stuffing the ballot boxes." Zeno, whom Governor Hunt appointed to the State Board of Transportation, was later indicted by federal prosecutors on charges related to his sale of land that was in the path of a state highway. He was later acquitted.

While I was serving as Governor Scott's military aide, Chuck Barber and I were sometimes at the Governor's Mansion one or two nights a week in our dress blues helping the Governor entertain dignitaries. After they'd all leave, Governor Scott would usually invite me to stay. "Ray, let's sit down and have a cigar and some white lightning," he'd say. Governor Scott liked cigars and white lightning. He said that a highway patrolman who worked at the mansion and lived up near North Wilkesboro would bring him a jar of white lightning every week. Another time, after Governor Scott left office and he was appointed to the Appalachian Regional Commission and had an office in Washington, I had a meeting in Washington and called Governor Scott to see if he might want to go to dinner with me and a friend. Scott said yes, but to stop by his office and we would go from there. My friend was Sherrill Faw from North Wilkesboro, and we were attending a builders' meeting in DC. When we got to Governor Scott's office, he said, "Let's have a drink before we go." Sure enough, he had a jar of white lightning under his desk, and we all had a drink. Sherrill asked Governor Scott where he got the white lightning, and the governor named a person from North Wilkesboro who was a friend of Sherrill's.

While Sherrill Faw and I were in Washington, we also had lunch at the White House, thanks to a young friend of mine whom I had hired during the Muskie campaign to work with the Young Democrats. After we closed down the Muskie campaign, this young man went to work for Jimmy Carter's campaign and ended up with a job at the White House. Sherrill and I were invited to lunch in a dining room especially set up to entertain contributors and supporters.

President's Message

J. Ray Sparrow

Beaucatcher Mountain, or better known as Asheville, or best known for that great association, Western North Carolina Home Builders, that's where the action is, that's where the home builders are putting it all together. I have just returned from a visit with this association and as you can see, I was impressed. Now, I know there are many strong home builders associations in this State and at this writing there are probably some that might be a little bit better, but I'll tell you this, Western North Carolina is breathing down their backs. In a city of a population of approximately 75,000, this association started out with a membership base this year of 125, its membership is already up to 143, but get this — their year end goal is 200 and I, for one, believe they will make it. Their committees are very active. They're active in BIPAC and they have another goal of building a permanent office this year for their association. At our last State-wide meeting they had 100% attendance of their board. As I travel around the State going from one meeting to another of this association, I sometimes wonder if it is all worthwhile but when I see what can be done by a dedicated president, an outstanding EO and an active membership, I know in my heart that our home builders associations are taking a giant step forward and our programs will be successful in spite of a few perennial foot draggers with negative attitudes. My hat is off to you, President McCurry, you have made my job easier and I look forward to my next stop with renewed enthusiasm.

Association activities around the State continue to be strong, your State staff and Executive Committee are wearing out the highways in trying to serve you. We just held the largest contractors licensing seminar ever with over 120 persons attending. Course I of the Builders' Institute was so large that we are going to have to hold two sessions, the Building Industry Political Action Committee is going good but we must never let our guard down until every member has sent in a minimum of $10. Have you sent in your fair share? If not, do it now. We are in the process of chartering two new associations, one in Whiteville and one in Forest City and there are others in the making. Our "Bring 'Em Back Alive" retention program is going well, but one word of caution — December and January have traditionally been big drop months for membership. This is why we have designed our retention program in hopes that it will minimize this drop. We have sent every local president a list of drops so that they can bring 'em back alive in February while their blood is still warm.

Did somebody mention this year's convention? It's going to be the greatest doggone shindig you will ever witness and I will tell you something else, if you haven't sent in your application, you had better get busy cause the way reservations are going, we're going to fill up those three little airplanes in a hurry. Nick De Mai, Sherrill Faw and myself have just returned from a State convention planning trip in the biggest convention city in the world, San Francisco. I don't have the space to go into the details but I will tell you that the sights like the Pacific Ocean, the Golden Gate Bridge, the Redwoods, the wine valley, Nob Hill and the cable car ride from the St. Francis to the cannery and fisherman's wharf are fantastically breathtaking. And, ladies, shopping like you will never forget, all for a low rock bottom price. It's once in a life time! I have had the pleasure of attending the past six State Conventions and I don't believe any one will touch the "fun city".

In closing, I want to say that our State Association wants to be of service to you. You are our best and only customers. Give us a call.

I would like to add a little bit about the North Carolina Home Builders Association. Before I served as the state president of the association in 1978 I served several terms as the association's lobbyist in the North Carolina legislature. I also started the association's Building Industry Political Action Committee (BIPAC). During my year as state president I helped double both the membership and the number of local HBA associations in the state. I would leave my office almost every day at noon

Raleigh North Carolina Chapter of the National Association of Women in Construction, Inc.

May 10, 1982

Reply To: Linda Douglas
c/o York Construction Company
P. O. Box 12085
Raleigh, N. C. 27605

Mr. Ray Sparrow
Sparrow Construction Company, Inc.
P. O. Box 33608
Raleigh, North Carolina 27606

Sparrow Construction Co., Inc.

MAY 13 1982

Dear Mr. Sparrow:

RECEIVED

Many, many thanks from the Raleigh Chapter of NAWIC! We were very proud to have you as our honored guest. Your program on Solar Energy was most informative and very well received by our members and guests.

We sincerely appreciate you taking time from your busy schedule to present it to us!

Sincerely yours,

Linda Douglas

Linda Douglas
Professional Education Chairman

/ld

cc: President Esther Jones

to visit a local association somewhere in the state, and visited all thirty-four associations many times.

The number of local associations within the state grew from fourteen to thirty-four while I was president. North Carolina also won the HBA National Membership Contest for the most new members that year. Today the North Carolina Home Builders Association has three full-time lobbyists and is one of the largest associations in the nation. It is one of the most effective political associations in both the state and the nation.

Another thing I was asked to do while working for Governor Scott was to fill in for him at several speaking engagements when he was tied up. One such engagement was in the town of Lumberton. I was to speak at the courthouse, but before the courthouse meeting I was to have dinner with some of the local leaders. During the dinner they gave me a list of things that they wanted the governor to do. Most of these leaders were from the Lumbee Indian Tribe, and most of the requests were things like getting jobs for their friends or releasing some of them from prison. I was glad to get to the courthouse after that. Incidentally, if you have ever been to the Lumberton courthouse, you might remember about fifteen or so pictures of judges hanging on the walls and all of their last names are "Britt." The following day, when I got back, I reported to Governor Scott and gave him the list of things the Lumbees wanted him to do. He looked at me, smiled, and said, "Just toss it in the trash can over yonder." Later that day, I found out that while I was in Lumberton, he'd been playing golf in Pinehurst. The governor liked to play golf. We would play sometimes at the Croasdaile Country Club in Durham. Croasdaile was about halfway between Raleigh and the Haw River, where he had a farm. This worked well because Chuck Barber was from Durham and a member of Croasdaile. A lot of my friends from Durham were members there.

In 1975 and 1976 I worked in the Jimmy Carter for president campaign, and the Democrats held a fund-raiser at Montague's Pond in

*Governor Hunt and I visiting the construction site
of Syracuse Plastics we built in Cary, NC*

Cary. Harvey Montague was a strong supporter of the Democrats, and his farm and clubhouse were often used for fund-raisers. I met Jimmy Carter's mother there at a fund-raiser the same year that Carter beat Ford for US president.

Also in 1976 Tom Bradshaw and I were asked to be cochairmen of the Wake County Jim Hunt campaign. Hunt was the lieutenant governor at the time and was almost a shoe-in for governor, having all of the Terry Sanford politicians, led by Bert Bennett of Winston-Salem, behind him. Hunt's workaholic hours were the stuff of legend, with aids, legislators, and others like me accustomed to receiving post-midnight or early-morning calls. The secular religion of southern governors such as Hunt was education, which is where Hunt focused most of his energies.

Tom and I set up a breakfast meeting every Monday morning for all the Wake County volunteers. We had about two hundred volunteers at every meeting, and we divided them into teams and had a contest to see which team could bring in the most money or new members for the Jim Hunt campaign. We were lucky to be in Wake County because Hunt often came by and spoke to his supporters—part of the reason I think Wake County workers raised more money for the Jim Hunt campaign than any other county. Tommy and I always had coffee before the meeting to go over what we were going to discuss. One morning I said to him, "Tommy, we had better get going because we only got about twenty minutes before the meeting starts." Well, Tommy was a very outgoing person who liked to be seen and heard, and he said to me, "Ray, you never go to a meetings early. If you want to be recognized, you always go late."

I remember another time later on in the campaign when Tommy and I went to the East Carolina University football stadium to a Jim Hunt rally. The place was packed, and after Hunt gave his speech, everybody was leaving. Tommy ran up and grabbed the microphone and started talking. There was hardly anyone left in the stadium when he got through. Tommy climbed down and asked me what I thought of his closing speech. I grinned and said, "Tommy, I thought that was the best leaving speech I ever heard."

Tom Bradshaw was a real leader. He became mayor of Raleigh and was appointed head of the Department of Transportation by Hunt. I might mention that Tom Bradshaw was also the mayor of Bald Head Island at one time. When we needed money for the Hunt campaign, Tom and I would go to Cliff Benson's office at Carolina Builders, a lumber company he owned in Raleigh that is now Stock Builders. Benson and several other businessmen pretty much controlled the Democratic Party's finances for many years. During one campaign, I remember the blacks in Southeast Raleigh coming to me and wanting their taxi money. They said that they used the money to take people to the polls. I asked Cliff about it, and he said that they gave the blacks fifty thousand dollars each election to get out the vote. I am not sure who really got the money, or if it was used to take people to the polls. That was in 1976, but it makes me wonder how much it costs to deliver the black vote today.

On another occasion, we held a Jim Hunt rally at the Wake Forest Country Club. I asked my sign man, Bobby Baker, who worked at the

Department of Motor Vehicles on New Bern Avenue, to put as many signs as he could between Raleigh and Wake Forest. At that time, most of the campaign workers like Bobby were state employees. I wanted to impress Hunt with all of those signs along US Highway 1 between Raleigh and Wake Forest. Unfortunately, Hunt flew to Wake Forest by helicopter and never saw a single one of the signs. A lot of shady things were going on, but the word was out not let Jim Hunt know about them. After Hunt beat David Flaherty by a wide margin and the campaign was over, Governor Hunt asked Tommy and I what we would like to do in his administration. Tommy wanted to be head of the Department of Transportation, and he was appointed right away. I said I would like to get back to my construction business since I had gone to the campaign office every day for about six months, including weekends. But that didn't happen. Since Tommy began his new job right away, working full time for the state, all of the loose ends of the campaign were turned over to me. When one of the campaign workers needed a job, they came to see me. When someone didn't like the way state government was run, they came to see me. During that time, as friend and political advisor to the governor, I made hundreds of phone calls and letters to state department heads and legislators trying to help out Hunt supporters.

The Department of Motor Vehicles was where we put the low-level campaign workers. Hunt hired over fifteen hundred new state employees during his term. Bobby Baker, the campaign sign man who worked at the DMV, was caught running a prostitution ring in the basement. Another employee, a nice-looking girl about twenty-five years old, called and asked to see me. When she came in and sat down, I asked about her problem. "I'm not going to sleep with him," she said. I asked "who" she was not going to sleep with, and she told me the name of her supervisor at the DMV. I assured her she wouldn't have to sleep with him, and that I'd take care of it. Things turned out well for her, because I found her

North Carolina
Department of Administration
116 West Jones Street   Raleigh 27611   (919) 733-7232

James B. Hunt, Jr., Governor

Jane Smith Patterson, Secretary

October 19, 1981

Sparrow Construction Co., Inc.

OCT 21 1981

RECEIVED

Mr. Ray Sparrow
Sparrow Construction Company
3815 Hillsborough Street
Raleigh, North Carolina 27611

Dear Ray:

Thank you very much for your letters of support, your words of encouragement and most of all, your steadfast belief that I would serve the people of North Carolina well.

Governor Hunt and Secretary Jane Patterson have asked me to serve as Policy Coordinator, heading up the new Office of Policy and Planning in the Department of Administration. This office has been established to provide policy support for the Governor's Office and to develop the data and other information for long-range planning. Our first major assignment will be to carry out the North Carolina 2000 project. Serving as Policy Coordinator will be a distinct challenge and one to which I am eagerly looking forward.

Again, thank you for helping to make this opportunity available to me. Your support was instrumental in my attaining this position and I deeply appreciate it. If I can ever be of any help to you, please let me know.

My very best wishes.

Sincerely,

Margaret C. Riddle
Policy Coordinator
Office of Policy and Planning

MCR/fb

Ray:
Words cannot express how much I have learned and how much I have enjoyed working with you. Thank you, again, for your friendship and your help— Marg.

I recommended many state employees

a better job in a different state department. Her supervisor was later indicted for misusing government funds. I had to take care of many situations like this with state employees, but I tried to make sure that Governor Hunt didn't know about the problems and hoped he wouldn't read about them in the paper.

In addition to having me handle all the state employees' problems, Governor Hunt appointed me to chair the state Savings and Loans Commission. This was when the housing business was going way up. It seemed that every little town wanted a new S&L. We had literally hundreds of applications for new S&Ls all over North Carolina, as many as two or three in each town. We had to study each one to see if it met state requirements. Later on, in the 1990s, most of them closed up when the housing industry went into a slump. During this period the Democratic Party bought the Goodwin House, a historic two-story home on Hillsborough Street, two blocks down from the state capitol to use as the state Democratic headquarters. The house was in really bad

North Carolina State Democratic Headquarters (The Goodwin House) Raleigh, NC

Dorton Arena, Raleigh, North Carolina

shape, inside and out, so the party came to me to help make it workable. I did all the work at cost without profit and sometimes at no cost. Later, I became a trustee on the Board of Directors and also was asked twice to serve as chairman of the Jefferson-Jackson Day ceremonies. The Goodwin House is still where the headquarters of the state Democratic Party is located.

Another thing I will never forget happened when I was attending a state convention during this period at the Dorton Arena building on the state fairgrounds. I was standing at one of the entrances with Jim Graham, a commissioner, and Bill Smith, another high-ranking state officeholder, watching the convention down below us. Bill said to Jim, "Have you ever been to a Republican convention?"

"No, why would I do that?" Jim asked

"You wouldn't believe the women," Bill said. "They're all dressed up, wear high heels, comb their hair real pretty—put on lipstick! And they smell good, too," he added. "But look down there at those Democratic women."

"What's wrong with those Democratic women?" Jim asked.

"Look at them! We call them the 'hairy-legged tow-sack women,'" he said. "They're wearing these great big flowery dresses that have no belts, probably because they can't find one big enough. Their dresses go down to their ankles, and they're wearing sandals and no hose—most of them don't shave their legs," he continued. "And don't get too close, because they don't smell so good!"

I didn't agree with Bill, and I said as much. My wife, Melba, and I had many Democratic women friends, and most of them looked like they had just stepped out of *Vogue*.

A couple of stories about Jim Graham. The colorful North Carolina Agriculture Commissioner was always a welcomed speaker at Democratic Party events during his four decades in that office. Not known for his articulate rhetoric, Commissioner Graham in his later years developed an awesome donkey bray. *Eee-HAW! Eee-HAW!*

On one occasion, the master of ceremonies called upon the commissioner to open the event. Most of the crowd knew what to expect, but two elderly ladies, sitting on the front row, did not. As the commissioner approached the podium, they bowed their heads ever so solemnly and were totally shocked when not a reverent prayer came from the commissioner's lips, but the deafening sound of a donkey's bray. As he descended from the podium, one of the ladies approached him and said, "Jim Graham, that is the worst thing I've ever heard you do. I will never speak to you again as long as I live."

Graham always described a "well-balanced farmer" as one who dribbled tobacco juice from both sides of his mouth. Jim told many funny stories.

Governor Jim Hunt and I became good friends. He got up early and worked late. I have over one hundred note cards and letters from him in his first term, and I don't know how many phone calls he made.

I remember one night about 11 p.m. I got a call from him asking for some advice on a bill in the legislature. I said, "Governor, why are you asking me when you got a great staff and lots of people around you who are much smarter than I am?" He said that was the problem. They only tell him the things they thought he wanted hear. He said, "You always tell it like you think it is, Ray."

Rob Christensen wrote in *The Paradox of Tar Heel Politics: The Personalities, Elections, and Events that Shaped Modern North Carolina*, "Once in office, Hunt's organization allowed him to quickly consolidate power. North Carolina's founding fathers, suspicious of concentrated power, had given the state one of the weakest chief executives in the country." North Carolina governors could not serve two consecutive terms, nor did they have veto power. Christensen continued, "Hunt changed all that. In 1977 he overrode the opposition of conservative Democrats to convince the legislature, and then the voters, to pass a constitutional amendment allowing governors and lieutenant governors to be elected to two consecutive terms. In the 1990s, Hunt pushed through a constitutional amendment that gave governors veto power."

Governor Hunt and I visited many Home Builders Associations together. Also, since my youth I had been involved in the Jaycees, which had about two hundred chapters across North Carolina, and I traveled from one end of the state to the other. At that time, you had to age out at thirty-five years old, but I spent another forty years in the North Carolina Home Builders Association, and traveled across the state again. It so happens that both of the organizations were very involved in local and state politics. Because I lived in Wake County, I was chosen to be an unpaid lobbyist for the N.C. Home Builders' Association for several years.

THE NATIONAL GUARD, 1951–1974

A word about my time in the National Guard. You may have noticed that a lot of the people I have mentioned so far served with me in the Guard. I was in the National Guard from 1951 until 1974. The last ten years, I served as company commander of the Thirtieth Infantry Division Headquarters Company. I find it interesting that so many of the people who served with me in the National Guard during the years I was active went on to become officers and leaders in local and national politics. I saw my friend Charles Scott become the North Carolina adjutant general under Governor Jim Martin. Gary Pendleton rose to the rank of a National Guard general and was elected to serve in the legislature. Major Tom Bradshaw was elected mayor of Raleigh and appointed secretary of the Department of Transportation by Governor Jim Hunt. Jim Harrington became a colonel in the National Guard and was also appointed secretary of the Department of Transportation by Jim Martin. Charles Heatherly rose to lieutenant colonel and served as deputy secretary to Harlan Bowles, longtime state treasurer. Heatherly served ten years under Bowles before becoming director of tourism for the state. Major Chuck Barbour was a military aide to Governor Scott and served as chairman of the Democratic Party. Major David Britt served as a military aide to Governor Scott. Colonel George Blaylock became the mayor of Dunn. Colonel Willis Hancock and Major Harry Vanderlindew served in the state legislature. General Claude T. Bowers was the North Carolina state adjutant general. Colonel Frank Danzet served on the Warren County Board of County Commissioners, and Major Roy Sowers served on the Sanford Town Council. Captain John Hatcher was a military aide to Governor Dan Moore. In 1958 General Charles Scott and I roomed together at Fort Benning, Georgia, while attending the Basic Infantry Officers Training Course. We were both second lieutenants at that time. We have been lifelong friends.

Additionally, many enlisted men in my unit went on to serve Wake County towns as mayors and councilmen. One of my top sergeants, Bob Cassell, served several terms on the Cary Town Council and became postmaster of the US Post Office in downtown Cary. Sergeant Jimmy Perry became the mayor of Wake Forest. Sergeant Joe Creech became the mayor of Garner, and John Alexander, who may have retired as a lowly sergeant in the Guard, has been elected from Wake County to the North Carolina senate for two terms. John comes from a long line of civic leaders. The Raleigh YMCA is named after his father, John M. Alexander Sr. Many local police officers, highway patrol officers, and

Ray shows off golf clubs presented to him by the men in his company when he retired as Company Commander, 30th Division Headquarters.

state department heads were also from the Thirtieth Infantry Division Headquarters Company.

I was with Leif Valand and Associates, Architects, and we designed the North Carolina National Guard headquarters building and several other National Guard buildings on Reedy Creek Road in Raleigh. I looked after the construction of this complex as well as several other National Guard armories around the state. Today the National Guard complex is so large it looks like an army post.

My construction company built several North Carolina National Guard armories and built many homes for the guard members.

As the division headquarters, we didn't take anyone but the best. I enjoyed every minute of helping these young men grow up and become outstanding business, civic, and military leaders. Many of them have remained lifelong friends. I am not saying, however, that every soldier in my unit was a saint. I am sure that I missed someone, but just about everyone in the outfit was involved in politics one way or another, even though they might not have held public office. Some were Democrats and some were Republicans.

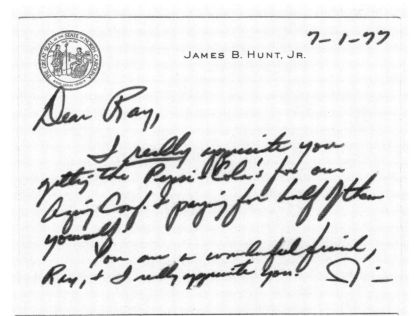

JAMES B. HUNT, JR.

7-1-77

Dear Ray,

I *really* appreciate you getting the Pepsi-Cola's for our Aging Conf. & paying for half of them yourself! You are a wonderful friend, Ray, & I really appreciate you!

JAMES B. HUNT, JR.

6-2-81

Dear Ray,

I've heard great things about your presentation to the Chamber of Commerce + the Wake delegation caucus. Super job. You're the best salesman I know. Warmest!

GOVERNOR JIM HUNT
POST OFFICE BOX 1980
RALEIGH, NORTH CAROLINA 27602

November 13, 1980

PERSONAL AND CONFIDENTIAL

Dear Ray,

I was deeply honored by the citizens of North Carolina in my re-election victory on November 4. This victory is a challenge to meet the high expectations of our people.

I want and need your advice on the strengths and weaknesses of our first administration and your thoughts on what matters I should give serious consideration to in setting up my second administration. Please be candid in your recommendations, as I want to know the broader view of how our state must function to meet such high expectations in the next four years.

Please mark your letter personal and private. I will be the only person to open and read it. Make it two pages or less. Please try to reply before Thanksgiving. Reply to Jim Hunt, P. O. Box 1980, Raleigh, North Carolina 27602.

Thank you for your continued friendship and counsel.

My warmest personal regards,

Sincerely,

Mr. Ray Sparrow, Sr.
P. O. Box 33608
Raleigh, N.C. 27606

Chapter Three

Second Term of Governor Hunt Campaign

IN 1979 GOVERNOR JIM HUNT ASKED ME to run his 1981 Wake County campaign for a second term as governor. We pretty much had the same people working in the campaign in 1979 as we had in 1975, except many more workers and lots more money. Jim Hunt was unstoppable. In the primary, his opponent was former governor Bob Scott; his general election opponent was I. Beverly Lake Jr. Hunt easily defeated both. Even though we didn't have Tom Bradshaw to help us in this campaign, we

had his wife, Mary Mac, to manage the campaign office. She was a great manager and a great people person. I often got credit for things Mary Mac did. The funny thing about this election was that Bob Scott said he was running for lieutenant governor, but in the end he filed to run for governor. Since we had been good friends, I spoke to him several times about his plans. I told him that since I was involved in the Hunt campaign I would do what I

Mary Mac Bradshaw

Campaigning in Wake County (Zebulon), April, 1980

could to help him, but I said that I thought nobody, including him, could beat Jim Hunt. After he filed for governor, I did not hear from Scott again. But a funny thing happened: I was assigned to escort Scott and his wife to the swearing-in ceremonies. I asked if he was mad at me and he said, "No, Ray, but you didn't have to work so hard!" Sometime later, he invited me up to his farm in Haw River to have a few sips of white lightning with him, and since then we remained good friends, until he passed away.

Another good friend who helped me in my personal campaigns and the many other campaigns I worked on was a young man named Pete Batton, now deceased. Pete was an employee of the State Paroles Commission, a great friend and one who would work around the clock. He not only knew all of the Jaycees around the state, but he knew almost all of the state employees in Wake County and the surrounding counties. Pete spent a lot of time in my construction company office trying to get

Scott friend on Hunt team

THE RALEIGH TIMES
Friday, December 7, 1979

J. Ray Sparrow

heads Wake campaign

By PAUL T. O'CONNOR
Times staff writer

Raleigh contractor J. Ray Sparrow has been named to head Gov. James B. Hunt Jr.'s re-election campaign in Wake County.

Sparrow has been active in Democratic politics for years, including earlier campaigns of Hunt's primary foe, former Gov. Robert W. Scott.

After the May primary, Sparrow said he hopes to visit Scott and "sit down, have a drink and still be good friends."

But until then, Sparrow said, he's "going to work like hell" to keep his friend out of the Governor's Mansion.

"We're good friends," Sparrow said of Scott. "But I really didn't have much of a decision to make in this campaign. I had already made my decision and given my word (to work for Hunt) when Bob Scott announced he was running for governor."

Sparrow, president of the Sparrow Construction Co., was co-chairman, along with state Department of Transportation Secretary Thomas W. Bradshaw, of Hunt's Wake campaign in 1976. The Hunt organization he helped build here four years ago has been resurrected for this campaign and is five or six months ahead of the last campaign in terms of organization, he said.

District and precinct organizations are in place, Sparrow said. Committees on senior citizens, state employees and other groups have been formed.

"We're going to have to give more emphasis to state employees because communication within state government is very poor. Sometimes just one issue, like whether or not there was a pay raise, is all you hear about. We've got to get out more information about the governor, try to get the positive side of the governor across," Sparrow said.

jobs for his parolees, but he also went to all of the Democratic Party events and as much as anyone helped me to get out the vote.

During this term, Governor Hunt appointed me chairman of the Teachers and State Employees Health Insurance Program. The legislature and the governor had decided to finance state employees' health insurance by going with a health maintenance organization (HMO) instead of the usual insurance companies. Since we did not have any HMOs in North Carolina at the time, several of our committee members and

Wake County Headquarters / 219 Hillsborough Street
Raleigh, North Carolina 27603 / Phone (919) 832-8304

WAKE COUNTY JIM HUNT NEWSLETTER

May 15, 1980   No. 6

* * *WE WON* * *   * * *WE WON* * *   * * *WE WON* * *   * * *WE WON* * *

CONGRATULATIONS to each and every one!! What a terrific victory in Wake County for all
of us who worked together as a team. In case you missed it, Governor Hunt got 62% of the
vote in our county. This is really super and we should all be very proud....but keeping
in mind all the hard work we have ahead of us in the fall. The general election will
take more work than the primary. However, after 2 months of rest, I know we will all
be ready to crank up again around August 1st.

Our primary week kick-off breakfast was a
success with 200 folks in attendance. Governor
Hunt presents County Chairman Ray Sparrow with
a birthday cake and a song at the breakfast.
From the look on Ray's face, it was certainly
a surprise. He had been so busy working in
the campaign that he had completely forgotten
that it was his birthday!!

* * * * * * * *

GOTV: Can you believe that every call was made?? That last week before the primary
folks were stuffed into this building. Every night's group wanted to make the most
calls but the Wednesday night "Tiger Team" of Becky Pittman, Dan Jones and Jack Setliff
won with 2,308 calls made in one night! Can't you just see all those fingers furiously
pushing all those buttons??!

To the hundreds of people who called and looked up telephone numbers, a hearty thank you!
They said it couldn't be done, but we DID IT! Elsie McDonald and Cynthia Wertz looked
up the most numbers, while Randolph Cloud made 2,605 telephone calls! Randolph was willing to do anything asked of him and for this we are so grateful. It has become second
nature to him to say "Hello, I'm Randolph Cloud from the Wake County Jim Hunt Headquarters..."

ELECTION NIGHT was such fun. Those of you who did not come by County Headquarters, we
are sorry as we missed you. It was FUN being together as precinct after precinct called
to report Governor Hunt's victory! Ray Sparrow got the results and posted them for all
to see with cheers after each result.

Hunt's second campaign

John Alexander brought refreshments; everyone fought for a piece of Rilma Ferguson's pound cake and Virginia Dolby's cheese straws. Dewanna Harris, Lynn Dolby, Pete Batton and Billy Fowler decorated the Hilton ball room for all the festivities. Donkeys were evident all over the room.

Governor Hunt smiles his victory smile and receives congratulations from former Governor Scott who graciously conceded and his remarks certainly showed what a true gentleman and statesman he is...not to mention a true DEMOCRAT! Truly, it was a night to remember for all persons concerned. None of it would have happened had everyone not done his share.

Everyone did so much, but to Billy Fowler who helped Peter Batton wrap Wake County up in Jim Hunt posters, we do thank you. What a fine job you did! This was made possible by Lucius JONES' generosity as he loaned them a brand new truck for a month. Lucius, has your truck been returned?? Bob Brooks and his crew put up 2 signs in all 76 precincts before 6:30 a.m. on Election Day. This takes real dedication and on that morning, a warm coat! Steve Glass was always so ready to make any number of posters for headquarters, Jeanette Woods ready to staple, Martha Agnew ready to fold, Martha Farmer transposing lists, Jane Donleycott calling and Fred Manley with his ability to organize. He could make order out of chaos in fifteen minutes flat. Elsie Bobbitt was so willing to help - as was everyone. All of you folks <u>made</u> the office run so smoothly.

LET'S TALK ABOUT THE FALL...After resting up from campaigning, we must be ready to go again and at full steam. Once again we will be calling on everyone to do more than before....push a little harder, smile a little broader, phone more folks, address more envelopes, more campaigning and work. Just remember how good the victory feels.

Our office will continue to work to get everything lined up for the fall. On May 30th we will be moving two doors down to 213 Hillsborough Street. The telephone number will remain the same. The Wake County Democratic Office will be joining us along with other democratic candidates. WE WILL BE IN TOUCH AROUND JULY 15TH. HAVE A GREAT SUMMER!!

JIM HUNT WAKE COUNTY HEADQUARTERS
219 Hillsborough Street
Raleigh, N. C. 27603

Bulk Rate
U.S. Postage
PAID
Raleigh, NC 27611
Permit #1364

MR AND MRS RAY SPARROW, SR.
P. O. BOX 33608
RALEIGH
NC 27606

I flew out to Denver, Colorado, to visit Kaiser-Permanente, an HMO that had started on the West Coast during World War II to take care of military people. Kaiser-Permanente was unique because every hospital under its coverage had two people in charge. One was a doctor and one a businessperson, which made sense a lot of sense to me; the doctor does what doctors are trained to do, and the businessperson does what businesspeople are trained to do. Fortunately, we were able to talk Kaiser into coming to North Carolina and handling our employees' health program, but with one hitch: since there were no laws in the state applicable to an HMO, I had to go before the legislature and get one passed.

We had one other problem. Since all of the members of this committee were businesspeople, we set the plan up on an 80/20 basis. The state would pay 80 percent of the cost and the employee would pay 20 percent of the cost, the practice of businesses at that time. The day after we set all the rules in place, we got all kinds of calls from state employees, legislators, and the governor, all raising hell about how much it was going to cost them. They were saying they wouldn't accept anything less than a 90/10 plan. What could we do but make the changes?

In 1991 Kaiser-Permanente opened an office on Blue Ridge Road, near Rex Hospital. It so happened that a good friend of mind named Dr. Dennis Zilavy was employed with Kaiser in Alaska. Dennis was an avid golfer and Alaska was no place for someone who wanted to play a lot of golf, so he decided to transfer to the Raleigh office and wanted to move to Cary to live. He and his wife, Larraine, who is as pretty and as nice a person as you would want to meet, came down from Alaska and bought a lot in the MacGregor Downs West subdivision in 1992. They asked me to build them a house. I drew some plans, met with them, they approved the plans, we agreed on a price, and they went back to Alaska while I was doing the construction. They came back in 1993 to move into the house. Until they came back in 1993, they had never seen the house until the day they arrived in Cary. They are still speaking to me. Matter of fact, we are not only good friends but at one time Dennis and I played a lot of golf together. Dennis finally dropped me as a golf partner because he was a very low handicapper and wanted to play with some real golfers, which was alright with me because I dropped him as a gin partner because he wasn't that good at cards. Dennis has been known to play as many as 240 rounds of golf a year. The weather doesn't seem to bother him. In June every year he still goes back to Alaska for a month to salmon fish. Dennis is retired, lives in the same house, and is still known to play a round or two of golf. Like his golf balls, Dennis is unaffiliated.

I was also serving on the Raleigh Chamber of Commerce board during this term, working on a committee to help finish the outer loop highway around Raleigh, now the inner loop. We were lobbying the Department of Transportation to get the loop finished. I had several friends like Tom Bradshaw and other longtime employees in the department who kept me informed; I'd helped some to get jobs and some I'd served with in the National Guard, so I thought I held a little clout there. The Chamber of Commerce committee recommended that the Highway Department do a plan for all the roads and highways to be built in the state for the next ten years. Then they'd take the plan to the legislature for funding. If your highway didn't make the plan, you would have to wait another ten years to get on the next plan. Well, guess what? I got a call from one of my friends in the Highway Department, and he said that Wake County did not make the ten-year plan. I immediately called Governor Hunt and reminded him how much Wake County had done for him. Later that day, I got a call back from the governor, saying Wake County was now on the plan. Sometimes that's how old-school politics worked.

Two other members of that Raleigh Chamber of Commerce committee were Dan Blue and Thad Eure Jr. Dan later became Speaker of the state house and is still serving in the North Carolina legislature. Thad's father, Thad Eure Sr., was secretary of state for fifty-two years. They called him "the oldest rat in the Democratic barn." Among other things, Thad Jr. owned a restaurant on Highway 70 near the RDU Airport called the Angus Barn, still very much a part of the scene today. The Angus Barn is not only noted as one of the best restaurants in North Carolina, but one of the best in the United States. Thad Jr. passed away a few years after he served on this committee and his daughter, Van Eure, took over the business. Van, a beautiful person and a good businesswoman, is involved in many charitable organizations in Wake County and the state. The Eures, lifelong Democrats, remain some of my friends.

Governor Hunt appointed me as chairman of the Division of State Construction. With all the problems with minority contracting, handicap codes, energy efficiency, and building code violations, this was more than a full-time job. I guess the governor couldn't find anyone who had nothing else to do!

About Tom Bradshaw: If you live in the Raleigh area, you've probably noticed that the last section of the highway, the "outer loop," was named the Tom Bradshaw Freeway. I would be remiss if I didn't say a few words about a person who has done as much for Wake County and the state of North Carolina as Tom Bradshaw. I have known Tom for a little over sixty years. Not only did we help get Governor Jim Hunt elected, but Tom and I worked on many other projects together. We were in the National Guard, the Jaycees, the YMCA board, and other political, civic, and business ventures together. We also played many rounds of golf, something we both enjoyed. Because of our work on the Hunt campaign and other activities, I feel that Tom and I together accomplished many great things for North Carolina. But Tom Bradshaw continued his career or service to the state far beyond mine. During Tom's five-year term as the head of the Department of Transportation, he secured legislation in 1977 to build a priority primary road from I-95 to Wilmington. Bill Heafner and Charlie Rose first got him appointments with the chairman of the US House Public Works Committee. The second step in the process was to secure approval to designate it as Interstate 40. By the time Tom Bradshaw's term ended in 1981, all of the right-of-way and thirty-two miles of interstate were opened to traffic.

Tom Bradshaw also secured additional interstate mileage for the I-40 bypass around Winston-Salem and the I-277 beltway around Charlotte. He also made it a priority to finish the Raleigh beltline and start the planning for the new outer loop, which would be I-540. The DOT also impaneled a blue-ribbon study committee chaired by former governor Dan K. Moore and reduced the Highway Department's workforce by twenty-five hundred people. Further, the legislature supported the department request in 1981 for a three-cent increase in salaries.

I could go on and on about Tom Bradshaw, how he began his career by starting Tom Bradshaw and Associates, opening an office in Cary. He first worked with Ed Woolner, representing Regency Park, and got IBM to Regency. Tom became Raleigh's youngest mayor, serving one term from 1971 to 1973. Shortly after, he took a position with First Boston Bank and had an office on Park Avenue in New York City. Tom traveled all over the United States in his new job. He also was elected to serve on the board of the National League of Cities (first North Carolina member) and on the Conference of Mayors Transportation Committee, where he served with Mayor Richard J. Daley of Chicago. In our early years Tom and I worked for the three developers that made Raleigh what it is today. Tom worked for Ed Richards, who did the original North Hills shopping center and office buildings. Ed and Tom, among other projects, built the North Ridge subdivision and Country Club. I worked with Willie York, who built Cameron Village and many other projects around Raleigh. Cameron Village was the first shopping center in the South. I also worked for Seby Jones, who developed Crabtree Valley and other major projects around Raleigh and the state. Although I am retired, Tom (a little younger than me) is still going strong.

Today, Tom Bradshaw is chairman of one of my favorite institutions, the Triangle YMCA Trustee Board. The YMCA, one of the biggest and I think best in the United States, is growing by leaps and bounds. It started out just in Wake County, but is now in many other counties. Like so many other young men, Tom Bradshaw started off in his early twenties as a Raleigh Jaycee. The Jaycees were always civic minded in their communities, but their main purpose was leadership training. Their motto was "Young Men Can Change the World." The Jaycees at that time was an all-male organization, and you aged out at thirty-five. Most of these men went on to be governors, legislators, mayors, and leaders all over North Carolina. I wonder where we are getting our leadership today? Unfortunately, it is hard to find a Jaycee organization in North Carolina anymore, and that's something that concerns me. Not many young people like Tom Bradshaw exist in our communities today.

STATE OF NORTH CAROLINA

OFFICE OF THE GOVERNOR

RALEIGH 27611

JAMES B. HUNT, JR.
GOVERNOR

November 21, 1977

Dear Ray:

I want to tell you personally how very much I appreciate your wonderful work in helping make North Carolina take the step forward we did on November 8. I know how hard you worked on it because of your aspirations for our state and your own personal commitment to progress.

Please know that I am deeply grateful for the leadership you have given to our people, and that I look forward to our continued work together for the good of North Carolina and the kind of future that the people of this state need and deserve.

Whenever I can be of personal assistance, I hope you will let me know. I look forward to seeing you soon.

My warmest personal regards.

Sincerely,

Mr. Ray Sparrow
Post Office Box 10035
Raleigh, North Carolina   27605

Thanks, Ray. I really appreciate you.

Sparrow Construction Co., I

DEC 6 1982

RECEIVED

STATE OF NORTH CAROLINA
BOARD OF TRUSTEES OF THE TEACHERS' AND STATE EMPLOYEES'
COMPREHENSIVE MAJOR MEDICAL PLAN

RAY SPARROW, SR.
CHAIRMAN

THOMAS J. HACKNEY, JR.
VICE CHAIRMAN

November 30, 1982

The Honorable Rufus L. Edmisten
Attorney General
Department of Justice
Post Office Box 629
Raleigh, North Carolina 27602

Dear Rufus:

The Board of Trustees has reviewed your letter of November 10, 1982, regarding Blue Cross and Blue Shield Corporation's responsibility to provide converted non-group health insurance to State employees who terminated employment between July 1, 1982 and September 30, 1982. Based on your opinion, the Board requests that you proceed to take the necessary steps to ensure that Blue Cross complies with the provisions of House Bill 983 and provides the non-group health insurance to these employees.

Thank you for your concern and attention to this problem. If we can be of any assistance, please let me know.

Sincerely,

Ray Sparrow
Chairman

MEMBERS
JAMES B. CHILDRESS   H. LEE CURRY   JOHN T. KING   ESTELL C. LEE
        MAYLON E. LITTLE   DONALD PATTERSON   DEWITT SULLIVAN

116 WEST JONES STREET—RALEIGH 27611   (919) 733-7061

STATE OF NORTH CAROLINA
OFFICE OF THE GOVERNOR
RALEIGH 27611

JAMES B. HUNT, JR.
GOVERNOR

November 12, 1982

Dear Ray:

I want to thank you for your participation in the
Democratic Party's televised response to President Reagan.

I am certain that your heartfelt, genuine comments,
together with those of all the others involved, made for an
excellent show that had a real impact on those who saw it.
I believe that the results on Election Day showed that
thousands of Americans share your feeling that we must
"correct the course."

I know you had to take time out from your day to
talk to our production crew, and I appreciate your willing-
ness to do that. It is people like you, who are willing to
stand up and speak up, that make this state and country
great.

My warmest personal regards.

Sincerely,

Mr. Ray Sparrow
1119 Queensferry Road
Cary, North Carolina 27511

Great job, Ray.

OT PRINTED AT GOVERNMENT EXPENSE

Chapter Four

My First Term in the House of Representatives

IN 1983 RUTH COOK DECIDED TO STEP DOWN from a seat in the North Carolina House of Representatives to take a full-time job with the state Utilities Commission. The Democratic Party placed their more important and smartest supporters on this commission. I think that all nine members of the commission at the time were Jim Hunt Democrats. Several of my political friends thought that I should run for Ruth Cook's seat. The Wake County Democratic Committee held an election and chose me to finish out Ruth's term.

I didn't do a whole lot that year except learn how the legislature was run. Though I already knew most of it, I soon found out that I didn't know the fine details, like how a handful of people ran everything and you voted along party lines or else. The Speaker of the House always had a couple of lieutenants who told you when and what to do. At the time, one of them was Billy Watkins from Oxford. The other was Bob Etheridge from Lillington in Harnett County. Bob and I got to be good friends, and he helped me later on when I ran for the state senate in Harnett County. Bob later served several terms in the US House of Representatives.

Dr. Robert K. Koger was chairman of the Utilities Commission from 1977 to 1988. Bob was appointed to the commission by Governor Jim Hunt.

Staff photo by Bob Bridges

J. Ray Sparrow beams Wednesday after selection by Wake Democratic Executive Committee

Sparrow is no newcomer to politics

By RICHARD HART
Staff Writer

J. Ray Sparrow may be new to public office, but the construction executive is no newcomer to the Wake County political scene.

Sparrow, 50, of Cary, was chosen by Wake Democrats Wednesday night to replace Rep. Ruth E. Cook in the state House in his first try at public office. He says he's been interested in politics since he worked in Adlai Stevenson's 1952 campaign for president — before he was old enough to vote.

But he is better known for his behind-the-scenes political work since then — as the chairman of Gov. James B Hunt Jr.'s re-election campaign, as co-chairman of Hunt's first run for the governor's seat and as an organizer and fund-raiser for Wake Democratic candidates going back 20 years. He also is Hunt's top political organizer in Wake.

"I've always been interested in that sort of thing, and I've found that by helping good candidates, we could get things done in our community that needed to be done," Sparrow said Wednesday in an interview.

Those years of contact with the political community — and the friends he's made and the work he's done for others — were instrumental in his selection Wednesday night.

"I wouldn't have a chance in this world if it wasn't for people helping me in this thing," he said.

Others who have worked with him praised Sparrow.

"He'll bring an extraordinary understanding of the political process to the job," said Rep. J. Alan Adams, D-Wake. "He is able to bring diverse views together for constructive purposes."

In particular, observers remarked upon his special interest in working for the average man.

"A lot of them (political organizers) forget the small people that really make the campaigns a success, who do the grunt work," said one Democratic observer who asked not to be identified.

"He's one of the rare birds who has a heart of gold and is sincerely interested in good government and trying to make things work for people."

Much of that comes from his background. Sparrow's father was a roofer in Norfolk, Va. Sparrow later moved to Durham and graduated from Durham High School.

"I didn't grow up in an affluent background at all," Sparrow said. After graduating, he went to work as a truck driver for a construction company, saved his money for a year, and then attended the School of Design at N.C. State University for two years — interrupted by another year of construction work.

After leaving school, he went to work for several architects and construction firms in the area before starting his firm, Sparrow Construction Co. Inc. He is president of the Wake County Homebuilders Association and a past president of the state organization.

He also has served on the board of directors of the N.C. Building Code Committee, the N.C. State Legislative Study Committee for Building Inspections, as chairman of the Downtown Housing Improvement Corp. and as chairman of the N.C. Savings and Loan Commission.

One state official, noting Rep. Cook's interest in housing issues, said that "Sparrow also is concerned, and knows the ins and outs of the housing industry."

Bob also served on the commission several other times. He is now president and executive director of Advanced Energy at NC State University. Some of the other people who served on the Utilities Commission were John Winters, Ruth Cook, and Howard Lee. John Winters also served on the Raleigh City Council and was a state senator, Ruth Cook served in the state legislature for several years, and Howard Lee was the first black mayor of Chapel Hill and served on many other state committees.

I started the 1984 session raring to go. Despite the time I spent on various committees to work out legislation that affected the entire state, the hometown bills kept me busiest. In that term I worked on legislation for retirement benefits for Cary's Fire Department and helped get a bill approved that allowed Holly Springs to build an airport. I was also successful in having a traffic light put in at Kildaire Farm Road and Maynard Road, and at the entrance to Apex High School. Getting a bill passed is not a matter of submitting it and calling for a vote. If it is a local bill, you have to make sure that other legislators from your county don't object, and you also have to work it out with the senators from your county. Otherwise you are dead in the water from the get-go.

In 1985 Jim Martin, a Republican, won the governor's office, and Jesse Helms defeated Jim Hunt for US senator. During the 1985 session, several pieces of legislation were aimed at Cary that affected towns throughout the state. I introduced the bill that has allowed conditional zoning, with developers now able to discuss possible land use when seeking to rezone. I also introduced a bill that allowed towns to accept payments in lieu of recreational land dedication.

On statewide issues, I occasionally was called a "maverick," although I preferred to think of myself as an individual. During my tenure, I voted what I thought was best for the people, even if it was different from party leanings. The last two years I was in the legislature, I submitted and had ratified twenty of twenty-three bills. They tell me that's some kind of a record. Of the three that did not pass, one was taken care of in the

10C...The Cary News, Cary, N.C., Wednesday, March 13, 1985

Health issue confronted

By GEORGE JETER
Staff writer

When health care costs account for "over 10 percent of the gross national product, it's getting out of hand" believes at least one state legislator.

Rep. Ray Sparrow of Cary is one of many North Carolina officials who have lent their time and support to Health Vote '85.

The campaign, which runs through April 15, is mixing informative meetings and media efforts with a public ballot. The effort is aimed at determining how people feel about the cost and quality of their medical care.

Health Vote organizers also want people to become aware of alternative ways of looking after their health, Sparrow said.

People need to know "what's happening in health care and the alternatives to bringing costs down," he added.

"We're not blaming the doctors and we're not blaming the hospitals " for high costs, Sparrow said. He feels most people simply do not know how to look for good buys in health care.

"If you're going to buy a car, you don't walk on a lot and pay the sticker price, you shop around," he said. Sparrow thinks medical care can be handled much the same way.

Sparrow first became interested in the rising costs of staying healthy when he realized the health insurance he bought for employees of his construction company had become "the largest part of my overhead."

He later served as chairman of the State Employees Health Program under former Gov. James Hunt. Such experience has led Sparrow to feel that the "cost of health insurance is almost prohibitive for a lot of people."

The Health Vote program and its parent organization, North Carolina Foundation for Alternative Health Programs, Inc., want to make a major point of stressing nontraditional systems between now and when ballots are counted in April.

The ballots will appear in newspapers and at area shopping centers such as Cary Village Mall. A tabulation of peoples' answers to the questions will be presented to the North Carolina Legislature.

Sparrow said his group will probably try to propose legislation based on results if any major trends appear in the answers. Ballots should start appearing around Cary April 1, according to Sparrow.

One way people can cut costs is by spending fewer days in the hospital

Ray Sparrow

per visit.

Patients at Duke Hospital in Durham for example, end up paying for research done by the university in their room bills, Sparrow said. "What you are paying for is the experiments they do. The public's paying for that," he said.

Another way to lower health costs is through a health maintenance organization, Sparrow added.

People joining these groups pay a regular flat fee which covers "preventive medicine," surgery and other doctors' care.

An advantage of using a health maintenance company is that the organization will work to keep its customers healthy so that bigger problems can be avoided. The organization will also use its purchasing power on hospitals and doctors to get better buys in services.

Since health maintenance groups make the local medical community compete for its business, this helps to lower local health costs for everyone, Sparrow said.

On the other hand the organization "may not give you an operation even if you need it," some people believe. This would be because the members' entire health program is covered by the flat fee. Therefore the organization is required to pay for all its customers other medical needs, Sparrow said.

The Health Vote backers are not pushing one side more than another in such questions, Sparrow said. Rather they are interested in finding out what ways the public wants costs cut — if any.

After all, "If people want to continue to spend their money on high escalating costs that's fine, but we want to know," Sparrow said.

Rep. Sparrow Stresses Education, Farming

BY LISA DREANO
Record Staff Writer

Rep. Ray Sparrow of Cary, a Democratic candidate for state Senate, stressed importance of improving state education and transportation, aiding farmers in economic straits, and other issues while campaigning this week in Dunn.

A free breakfast for Sparrow will be held Saturday, April 12, at 8 a.m. at Wade's Restaurant in Coats. The breakfast is being held by Carson Gregory, Sam Stephenson, and J.C. Lucas. Everyone is invited to come out for breakfast and a chance to meet with Rep. Sparrow.

Rep. Sparrow has served two terms as a Democratic legislator representing the 62nd district. He is running for the state Senate in the 14th Senatorial District which includes Lee, Harnett,

Continued on page 14

REP. RAY SPARROW

This article continued on next page

Rep. Sparrow Stresses Education

Continued from page 1

and Wake counties. Sparrow stresses that "politics is his vehicle, not his purpose."

Sparrow is a Cary businessman, chairman of the Downtown Housing Improvement Corporation, chairman of North Carolina Savings and Loan Commission; president of Sparrow Construction Co., Inc., and past administrative national director of the United States Jaycees. He is on the Board of Directors of the Raleigh Chamber of Commerce and a member of the Cary Chamber of Commerce.

His honors have included Cary's Outstanding Young Man of the Year, N.C. Home Builder of the Year, life member of the N.C. National Guard Association and of the N.C. Jaycees, and the N.C. Distinguished Service Award. He is married to the former Melba Truelove of Apex and they have three children; Ray Sparrow, Jr., a Washington, D.C. attorney; Michele Sparrow, vice president of Southern Data, Inc. of Raleigh; and Melanie Sparrow, a senior at N.C. State University.

Sparrow emphasized his past experience in the legislature which he said has given him an understanding of the issues that face North Carolinians today. He said that due to the cuts that will be precipitated by the Gramm-Rudman legislation and possible elimination of revenue sharing, the state must be especially careful in how it spends its money over the next few years.

One area where he would like to see careful spending and promote excellence is that of education. He said that there are more than 800,000 North Carolinians with less than an eighth grade education. He added that N.C. has a record high number of dropouts. He said that he would like to see an increased emphasis on vocational education, would like to push career development for teachers and administrators, and would like to see a reduction in class sizes.

"We're faced with tremendous needs and limited dollars. We need to put our dollars to the best use. I would like to see some of those dollars used to improve education in our state. Our future lies in the education of our leaders of tomorrow. We need to continually seek to improve our system of education," said Sparrow.

Sparrow is presently serving on the state's legislative Research Study Commission on Railroad Property, outdoor advertising, state infrastructure needs, and as chairman of the N.C. Council on Interstate Cooperatives. He also serves on committees on banks and thrift institutions, constitutional amendments, corrections, finance, housing, judiciary, small business, transportation, and law enforcement in the General Assembly.

Transportation is another large area that Sparrow would like to see improved.

"Transportation, like education, has been a catalyst for the expansion of our existing industries and influx of new ones. Our highway system is short $200 million each year of just maintaining the road system. We have 75,000 miles of state maintained roads. We have more state-maintained roads than any other state. We need to try to maintain our road and improve our road system," said Sparrow.

Sparrow said that he is also very concerned about the economic plight of North Carolina farmers. He said that there are about 75,000 North Carolina farmers. In the past five years, between 3000 and 4000 farms have failed each year, he said. He said that much of this situation is due to the soaring machinery prices, drop in food prices, and other factors.

"Agriculture is one of our main industries. It is a backbone of our state. We need to explore ways to try to help the farmers maintain their farms. We can look at ways to develop alternate crops, and promote diversification of farmland. We need to push tax programs to allow farmers to obtain a decent living. We also can look into developing new markets for farmers," said the representative.

Sparrow said that he believes that his legislature experience would greatly aid him as a state Senator. He said that he has a wide knowledge of Harnett, Lee, and Wake counties and would like to utilize his knowledge and experience as a state Senator.

Conditional zoning is perfect for Cary

The approval of the conditional zoning process by the N.C. General Assembly last week is a major breakthrough for fast-growing Cary.

Under the new bill introduced by N.C. Rep. Ray Sparrow of Cary, developers and landowners now can present site plans when seeking a rezoning request from the Cary Town Council.

In the past, under the contract zoning regulations, developers could not legally even hint at the possible use of the site when requesting a zoning change from the town. Frequently, this placed everyone from developers to the town council to concerned neighbors in a difficult situation.

With Cary finishing in sixth place in new construction projects across the state during 1984, requests for rezonings have dominated the town council's attention for months. An equally incredible amount of time is spent by the town's employees in processing and studying these rezoning requests.

The scenario at the public hearings on the requests is much the same every month. The developer presents his reasons for the rezoning request, carefully avoiding his exact plans for the property, but citing reasons such as "best use for the property" and other ambiguous phrases.

Residents who have homes that abut the property naturally are concerned about what is going to be located nearby. They are worried about property values, increased traffic volumes, their children's safety and various other problems that might occur if the rezoning is approved.

And, the town council is caught in the middle, wanting to be responsive to the residents of the town and, at the same time, wanting to allow quality development into the town.

Everyone is dealing with a great number of unknowns, making the process bulky, frustrating and time-consuming.

The new conditional zoning law should eliminate some of the existing problems.

The developer will be able to put all his plans right on the table, up front, for the council and residents to examine and question.

The new process will not eliminate conflict and debates, but it was not intended to do so. However, it will allow the debates and the conflicts to have some real meaning and substance, with the developer, the town council and the residents knowing exactly what they are dealing with.

We look for the new legislation to allow for some intelligent debate on the rezoning requests with some top-quality decisions made after all the questions and problems have been handled.

The bill appears to be made for a boom-town like Cary.

Bill introduced to permit new Raleigh zoning

Rep. J. Ray Sparrow, D-Wake, has introduced a bill in the General Assembly that would permit in Raleigh conditional zoning — in which developers show the City Council their plans for developing land they wanted rezoned.

The bill, filed at the request of the Raleigh City Council, would allow developers to give detailed descriptions of their building and landscaping plans, and allow the city to require that the plans be followed, Sparrow said. The bill was assigned Tuesday to a House local government committee.

Raleigh now does not permit petitioners to divulge plans before rezoning because the courts have ruled that local governments cannot pressure a developer to agree to a certain project.

The conditional zoning concept included in Sparrow's bill would not be affected by the court rulings because developers would still have the option of seeking rezoning under the current method.

Sparrow of Cary said the bill was supported by both developers and neighborhood groups because it would narrow some of the broad zoning categories that now allow many types of development on a given location. Neighborhood groups dislike the broad categories because they make it impossible to know what type of development will occur on a tract after it is zoned, Sparrow said.

Some developers dislike the broad zoning categories because they generate opposition from neighborhood group members who worry that a developer may propose one type of project and then build another.

Sparrow's bill would amend the city charter to allow the city to "provide for the creation of conditional use zoning districts and overlay zoning districts and transitional zoning regulations in addition to general use districts."

"The overlay option would let you show the city council exactly what you're going to build . . . And whatever you draw (on the plans), you have to build," Sparrow said. "There would be no deviation."

regular budget bill, and the other two were still being researched. I think more legislators should speak out. In my opinion, one of the shortfalls of the North Carolina General Assembly is the lack of representation from the business community. We don't have enough businesspeople who have had to make a payroll. Without that experience, they just don't have an understanding of what a dollar is worth.

My time in the House was not all wine and roses. Sometimes when I didn't vote along party lines I caught hell, but as I've said, I believe you should always do the right things for the right reasons. There was one bill that I will never forget. The *News & Observer* ate me alive for fighting this bill. It was a local city of Greensboro bill about minority contractors introduced by Representative Herman C. Gist. Gist was black. He introduced a bill that said that if a government agency got bids on government work, they did not have to take the lowest qualified bidder, so if a contractor bid one hundred thousand dollars on a government project and a minority contractor bid two hundred thousand dollars, the agency could decide to give the project to the highest bidder. State law at the time required that state and local government take the lowest responsible bid on public projects costing thirty thousand dollars or more.

One of the problems with this bill was that most larger cities had one or more blacks on the councils and the rest of the members were very liberal, which meant that they could give a bid to a minority contractor and the taxpayers would have to foot the bill. The other thing was that this was what we called a "run-on" bill, which meant that if it passed as a local bill, they would run it statewide. But the real problem for a legislator, since this was a local bill, was that, according to an unwritten rule, you don't speak out against another county's bill. You could vote against it but not speak against it. The debate went on for several weeks, and the *News & Observer* stayed on my case for fighting a local black bill, contending that I had a conflict of interest because I was a contractor. Interestingly, at that time I had not done any government work. I was mostly building houses.

Wake lawmaker's interests draw fire after House vote

By MICHAEL WHITELEY
Times staff writer

Rep. J. Ray Sparrow's role in the General Assembly as the voice of North Carolina builders drew fire Monday from a fellow House member who said Sparrow gutted a bill that would have boosted the hiring of minority contractors by the city of Greensboro.

"Since I've been here in the General Assembly, I've heard only one individual get up on the floor of the House and say he was acting for special interests," said Rep. Herman C. Gist, D-Guilford. "Mr. Sparrow made that statement. This is unprecedented. I haven't seen a local bill gutted by legislators from outside the county before," Gist said.

Sparrow, a Cary builder and Wake Democrat, told the House of his interests and said in earlier debate that his experience as a contractor put him in a good position to see the problems with the controversial bill.

Following Gist's comments, the House voted 73-30 to approve a bill substantially weakened by Sparrow's amendment.

Without the amendment, Sparrow said the bill was dangerous to the free enterprise system because it waived the state's competitive bidding laws.

Citing Raleigh's program of training minorities to bid projects, he said the Greensboro bill could spread to the rest of the state.

"Everybody up here represents a special interest and they vote that way," he said. "I can tell you how everyone is going to vote on almost every issue. They vote for the people they represent.

"I represent contractors and I'm a builder . . . and I believe in the free enterprise system," Sparrow said.

Sparrow said the city of Raleigh has let $15 million in construction contracts to minorities by assigning city workers to train the companies in preparing bids.

He said his company does not stand to benefit from the Greensboro bill.

The bill, filed by Greensboro lawmakers, would have allowed the city to develop requirements for participation by minorities and women in city contracts.

State law currently requires that state and local government take the "lowest responsible" bid on public projects costing $30,000 or more.

Gist's bill would have allowed the city to refuse a bid that did not meet its standards for participation by minorities and women. In a vote that evenly divided the Wake County delegation, the House passed an amendment by Sparrow that stripped the key provision from the bill.

The amendment further banned the city from making any minority hiring requirement "a condition precedent to the award of the contract."

Reps. Daniel T. Blue, Margaret

Article continued next page.

(Peggy) Stamey, and Betty H. Wiser voted against the amendment. W. Casper Holroyd, Aaron E. Fussell and Sparrow, the delegation's three white males, voted for the amendment.

Blue chairs the N.C. Legislative Black Caucus and is the county's only black lawmaker. All six are Wake Democrats.

Gist voted against the bill during the test vote Monday night and said he will work to defeat Sparrow's amendment before the House takes a final vote today.

"With the amendment, it doesn't mean anything," Gist said. "The bill does absolutely nothing."

Sparrow, who owns Sparrow Construction Co., has played a key role in several Raleigh bills involving developers this session. He forged a compromise between the city and developers on bills allowing the city to charge developers impact fees to help build roads and parks their subdivisions make necessary.

He also smoothed the way for Monday night's passage of a bill allowing the Raleigh City Council to regulate the cutting of trees on private property. Sparrow is only member of the Wake House delegation whose district is excluded from the city of Raleigh.

Rep. Stamey said Sparrow has played a valuable role in working compromises on development-related issues, but would not comment on his involvement in the Greensboro bill.

J. Ray Sparrow
'I believe in free enterprise'

"It is unusual for us to get involved in another county's local bills," she said.

Both House and Senate rules ban lawmakers from voting on any issues from which they might benefit.

But legislators are allowed to decide whether his stake in the legislation could influence his vote. Sparrow, who is serving his first full term in the House, said he chose to challenge the Greensboro bill because no one else would.

"I could have sat there and kept my mouth shut, but I'm not like that," he said.

Article continued from previous page.

I could not tell the *News & Observer* that Liston Ramsey, who was Speaker of the House, had come to me and asked that I fight the bill. Ramsey said that it was one of the worst bills he had seen come before the legislature. I'd asked him why he was asking me to fight the bill when he had all his lieutenants and other democrats to fight it. He'd said that they could not find one Democrat to fight this bill because they might lose the black vote in their district. I decided to fight the bill, and it failed in a landslide. As of today, such a bill has never been brought up again. Needless to say, I suffered the consequences later on. Because I didn't toe the line, I had many more tough battles in my final term. You could vote against a black bill but not speak against it.

When Governor Jim Martin came into office, which was my second term in the legislature, he appointed Jim Harrington as head of the Department of Transportation. Since Jim and I had been good friends in the National Guard and both had connections with Walter Davis, Harrington asked me to introduce a highway funding bill in the House. I thought it was a good bill, so I rounded up enough votes to get it passed, but just barely. Harrington's wife, Ann, sat behind me in the legislature. They still live on Bald Head Island.

That was in 1987. At that time you could get things passed in the North Carolina House even though the Speaker, Liston Ramsey, may not have always been for it. Liston had served in the legislature for forty years and his last eight years as Speaker of the House, but in 1987 there was a coup led by Representative Joe Mavratic from Tarboro to try and unseat Liston in the 1988 House election. The House at that time was sort of split up. I happened to know most of the Mavratic team, and you could get their support on some bills if Ramsey was against them. I had enough support on the highway bill to barely pass it. Actually Mavratic did become Speaker of the House in 1988, ousting Liston Ramsey.

My seat mate at that time was a good friend named Casper Holroyd. This was Casper's first term. Needless to say, there was a lot of infighting

STATE OF NORTH CAROLINA
OFFICE OF THE GOVERNOR
RALEIGH 27611

JAMES G. MARTIN
GOVERNOR

May 8, 1985

The Honorable J. Ray Sparrow
House of Representatives
State Legislative Building
Raleigh, North Carolina 27611

Dear Ray:

A sincere and grateful thanks to you for your
vote against tabling Ray Warren's amendment to
exempt the elderly from the sales tax on food.
Hopefully, your stand on this will help our
efforts presently under way to accomodate some
relief for the elderly in the legislation before
the Senate Finance Committee.

I also wish to commend you for your stand in
committee and on the floor for letting the people
vote on the executive veto amendment. Although
our effort was unsuccessful, we were able to build
a record for future consideration.

Again, thank you very much.

Sincerely,

James G. Martin
Governor

Changes give city tree bill better chance

By MICHAEL WHITELEY
Times staff writer

Raleigh officials and Wake County lawmakers may be nearing common ground in the city's bid for the right to ban the removal of trees on private property, officials said this week.

"I think it's possible that something can be done," said Rep. J. Ray Sparrow, D-Wake.

Sparrow had lead delegation resistence to a request earlier this session by Raleigh officials for the power to regulate the removal of all trees on private property.

Sparrow, a Cary builder, said the ordinance would violate the rights of property owners and allow improper intrusion by government into what should be private affairs.

Through its planning and zoning processes, the city already has the power to require that new developments preserve areas for "green space" and vegetative buffers.

But Mayor Avery C. Upchurch last week asked Sparrow to consider a compromise version of the bill that would allow the city to regulate trees in specific areas.

The bill would allow city to enact its own ordinance to regulate the "planting, maintenance, removal replacement, grading and preservation" of trees:

- On slopes graded 15 percent or steeper.

- In the designated federal flood plain.

Rep. Ray Sparrow
'something can be done'

- Of a diameter of 82 inches or greater.

- Considered historic.

The bill would require 180 days review by the city before a tree could be removed in one of the designated areas.

Upchurch said officials have not yet worked out the definition of historic. That is expected to be settled during a public hearing, if lawmakers give city officials the right to draft an ordinance.

"I can see where we may have to do something in areas that we need to protect from erosion," Sparrow said. "There are still some elements of the ordinance I have problems with. But I certainly like this bill more than the last one."

Sparrow said this week he would be reviewing the bill with other lawmakers and with Raleigh developers.

Upchurch said he also plans to lobby developers to muster support for the tree ordinance.

between the Democrats and Republicans with the new administration taking over. Since this was a Republican bill, the Democrats made a motion to adjourn on a Friday afternoon, a well-known technique they used to keep the bill from going to a vote, especially if it looked like it might pass. When I introduced the bill on the following Monday, the Democrats had twisted enough arms and legs over the weekend that the bill didn't have a chance.

My friend Casper said he couldn't vote for my bill because he'd been warned that if he did, he would never get to be a chairman of any committee. Well, Casper, who was also my seat mate in my second term, never got to be a chairman anyway because he didn't get elected to a second term. The irony here is that a week after the bill was voted down, the Democrats introduced the same bill, but with their name on it, and it passed unanimously. All I can say is, that's politics.

Another interesting person with whom I was in daily contact in the legislature was James C. Green, a Bladen County representative who served as Speaker of the House from 1975 to 1976. Jimmy Green, a colorful speaker, had been instrumental in getting Martin elected when Green threw his support behind Martin after losing a bid himself for governor in the 1984 primary. Unfortunately, Green had his share of legal trouble, most of it related to his tobacco warehouse business dealings. He was convicted of income tax fraud in 1997 and sentenced to thirty-three months of house arrest. Green died in February 2000.

There are all kinds of stories about Lieutenant Governor Jimmy Green. One I remember is that someone knocked on Jimmy's front door one evening. His wife answered the door and the person asked her if this was Jimmy Green's house. His wife said, "Yes, just put him on the couch. Everybody else does."

The 1988 election for governor had three Democrats running for the nomination in the primary. They were Eddie Knox, a longtime Democrat from Charlotte; Lieutenant Governor Jimmy Green; and the state

STATE OF NORTH CAROLINA
OFFICE OF THE GOVERNOR
RALEIGH 27611

JAMES G. MARTIN
GOVERNOR

July 9, 1986

The Honorable J. Ray Sparrow
North Carolina House of Representatives
Room 1315, Legislative Building
Raleigh, North Carolina   27611

Dear Ray:

It is with great respect that I salute your vote on July 8, 1986, to restore the basic concept of the compromise fashioned by the Lieutenant Governor and me to provide roads for the future of North Carolina. Your courage in standing firm for your own convictions against substantial pressure on an issue of this magnitude reflects your concern for the real needs of our State and holds promise for the congenial relationship between the Legislative and Executive branches of government which we both seek.

I am hopeful that the final resolution of the roads issue will reflect the bi-partisanship out of which the Senate Committee Substitute arose. Your strong support on Tuesday makes that outcome more likely.

I congratulate you and thank you for your bi-partisan support of government in the interest of the people. My only regret is that your retirement from the General Assembly this year will limit our opportunities to work further together over the coming years.

Yours very truly,

James G. Martin

jy

Ray - you took a particularly strong stand, for which I'm grateful. That close 57-60 vote on your amendment set the stage for victory. Thanks.

attorney general Rufus Edmisten. Rufus won the Democratic primary nomination. Eddie Knox was so upset he switched parties and worked for Jim Martin, the Republican nominee from Charlotte. Jimmy Green was also mad, so he supported Jim Martin. Most folks say that because of Knox's and Green's support, Jim Martin, the Republican, won the election, and not Rufus Edmisten.

By the way, my seat mate in my first term was Al Adams. Al was rated as one of the most effective members of the North Carolina House of Representatives. He served ten years in the House and was a partner in the ex-governor Terry Sanford's law firm. Al won just about every award you could imagine in Wake County and North Carolina. He was inducted into the Raleigh Hall of Fame "in recognition of his accomplishments in Law, public service, and civic leadership," and as a "powerful advocate for equality and justice, arts and education and cultural institutions, serving the City of Raleigh and the State of North Carolina." Even though Al was probably the most liberal person in North Carolina, and I was leaning more to the right, Al taught me a lot about the legislature and always gave me great advice. That's the way the legislature worked back then. Al and I became good friends and remained so for the rest of his life. I feel fortunate to have been his seat mate and his friend. I had many Democratic friends like Al back then. I still do.

Chapter Five

My Second Term in the House

IN 1985 I RAN FOR MY SECOND TERM in the House. The House seat represented most of western Wake County. An experience that I will never forget was visiting eight black churches in two weekends. If you've never visited a black church, you should do it at least once. Johnny Byrne, who is the mayor of Fuquay and had been for about twenty years then,

The North Carolina Legislative Building, Raleigh, North Carolina

asked if he could help me in my campaign. I'd helped his father, Tommy Byrne, get on the Wake County Board of Commissioners. Incidentally, Tommy pitched for the New York Yankees back in the old days when they always won, and I have been a Yankees fan since I was a little boy. Johnny lined me up with a black man from Fuquay by the name of Twice who owned the black funeral home there. They set up a schedule for me to visit most of the black churches in that end of the County—two Sundays, four churches each. Now, you might wonder how I could visit four churches in one day, but the black churches are an all-day affair. It's not like church where you go to at eleven and people start walking out at twelve. In the black churches the preacher might preach an hour or two; then, after church services, there would be a cookout that might last until dark and maybe more preaching that night. It was about the same at each church. All of the women were dressed in white, and all of the men were dressed in black. If you got to the church when the music was playing, it was a special treat. Usually, when we arrived there'd be a church political person who met us at the side door. You'd pay him two hundred dollars in cash. I figured the money went to the church, but I didn't know for certain. Anyway, he would seat you on the front row and the preacher would look down at you and keep on preaching until he decided it was time for you to speak. He would then say something like, "God, it is time to take a political break. We got Ray Sparrow with us today." I'd get up, give my pitch, and then leave. We'd then drive about seventy miles an hour to get to the next church, lucky if we didn't have a wreck or get arrested. In the afternoon, we'd have some more great food, listen to some more music, and go again. I saw some of the best singers and heard some of the best organ music that I have ever seen or heard since, better than what you see on television.

All the mayors in District 62 endorsed me for my second term in the State House. District 62 is the largest legislative district in Wake County. At that time, the district had a population of over fifty-two thousand.

Mayors
for
Sparrow

We are supporting Ray Sparrow for the House of Representatives because he is well qualified to represent the people of Wake County. Ray is in touch with the problems that the communities in Wake County face, including the need for better housing, improved education, and increased fire and law enforcement services.

Having been raised in a rural town, Ray understands the desire of communities to maintain their individual way of life. He is also keenly aware of the need for clean water, wastewater treatment plants, and improved roads and streets to provide for stable growth.

A caring person, Ray knows the need for providing support for essential human services. As a member of the Wake County Education Foundation, Ray is dedicated to the importance of providing for the best education in Wake County. Ray's reasonable approach to solving problems results in practical solutions; solutions we can afford to live with.

We urge you to vote for Ray Sparrow for the North Carolina House of Representatives on November 6.

Sincerely,

ALFRED M. JOHNSON
Mayor - Town of Fuquay-Varina

WILLIAM A. WILDER, JR.
Mayor - Town of Knightdale

GERALD W. HOLLEMAN
Mayor - Town of Holly Springs

HAROLD RITTER
Mayor - Town of Cary

LARRY M. JORDAN
Mayor - Town of Apex

JOHN WATKINS
Mayor - Town of Garner

All of the mayors endorsed Ray in his run for a second term

Back at the Legislative Building, I got involved in the state Housing Finance Agency. When I had served as chairman of Raleigh Downtown Housing Cooperation (DHIC) a few years before I served in the legislature, we'd built the first two low-income houses in Southeast Raleigh, so I knew a little about low-income housing.

The North Carolina Housing Finance Agency had also built a few low-income houses, but they had no builders on their board, just bureaucrats. I was asked to get involved to try to get things moving. I had a friend, Ralph Forest, who was a member of the Carolina Country Club, so I asked him if he could use his membership to get reservations for a luncheon meeting for the N.C. Housing Finance Agency. I'd do the rest, inviting some members of the legislature and some statewide builders. Ralph made the luncheon arrangements with the club, and we had a great meeting. Unfortunately, the club was not as happy. Ralph Forrest called me the night after the luncheon and inquired as to who attended the luncheon. I told him it was Lieutenant Governor Jimmy Green; Howard Lee, who was the first black mayor of Chapel Hill; a few of his aides; and some builders. Ralph said that the club had threatened they'd take his membership away since their covenants didn't allow black members.

I didn't even attempt to say that Howard Lee wasn't a bit interested in becoming a member of the Carolina Country Club. I just told Ralph to tell them to go right ahead and I'd set up a meeting with Senator Jesse Helms, Howard Lee, Jimmy Green, and several other legislators to talk about why Carolina Country Club wasn't integrated. Ralph called me back about an hour later and said not to say anything more about it, that the club had said they would not take away his membership. Coincidentally, Frank Daniels Jr., whose family owned the *News & Observer* at that time, was also a member of the Carolina Country Club, and I was chairman of the MacGregor Downs Country Club Board of Directors. Maybe Frank Daniels Jr. was like me and did not know that our clubs

P.O. Box 2185
419 North Boylan Avenue
Raleigh, N.C. 27602
919-755-6158

Downtown Housing Improvement Corporation

BOARD OF DIRECTORS

Don Kennedy
Bass, Nixon & Kennedy
    Chairman
Clarence E. Lightner
President, Lightner Funeral Service
    Vice Chairman
Minetta Gaylor Eaton
Retired Principal
    Secretary/Treasurer

J. R. Adams
Adams-Bilt Homes
Edna Earle Blue
Real Estate
Donald H. Carpenter
Sr. Vice President
First Citizens Bank
William Cox
North Hills, Inc.
Leotha Debnam, Sr.
Clergyman
David Falk
Tucker & Falk Real Estate
Charles Murphy
NC State University
Sheila A. Nader
League of Women Voters
Elton C. Parker
Nationwide Insurance
Grady Perkins
Spaulding & Perkins, Ltd.
Lulu Harris Robinson
Assistant Professor
St. Augustine College
Alton Strickland
Raleigh Paint & Wallpaper
John Stokes
Community Resident

Frederick J. Whitney
    Executive Director

May 22, 1980

Home Builders Association of Raleigh
    and Wake County
1301 Annapolis Drive
Raleigh, NC   27608
Attn: Nancy Kaufman

Dear Ms. Kaufman:

At its May 22, 1980, meeting, the Board of Directors
of the Downtown Housing Improvement Corporation
unanimously passed a resolution supporting the
nomination of former DHIC Board Chairman J. Ray
Sparrow as North Carolina Homebuilder of the Year.

Ray Sparrow has been, and continues to be, a major
factor in the success of the DHIC. His two terms
as Chairman helped to form the foundation of the
Corporation. His personal interest in low and
moderate income housing at a time when it was not
a popular concept shows that he is truly a person
who is concerned with the housing needs of all
people in North Carolina.

It is with great pleasure that the DHIC Board has
the opportunity to publicize Ray's dedication to
fair and affordable housing for all people and his
long service to the Downtown Housing Improvement
Corporation.

Sincerely,

Don C. Kennedy
Chairman

Frederick J. Whitney
Executive Director

FJW:pjb

HOWARD N. LEE

P.O. BOX 25453
RALEIGH, N. C. 27611-5453

October 24, 1991

Mr. J. Ray Sparrow
1119 Queensferry Road
Cary, N. C. 27511

Dear Ray:

Please accept my deepest and most sincere appreciations for signing the letter of invitation and for being a sponsor for the Friends of Howard Lee reception. I consider it an honor to have had a person of your stature as a member of the sponsoring team. Ray, your friendship and support means a great deal to me and will be among my most cherished holdings for many years. If I can help you in any way, please don't hesitate to call.

I was very pleased with the attendance at the reception. The fact that forty-five (45) people were willing to take time from a Sunday evening to attend a reception was quite gratifying. The gross amount of money generated was $ 4,410 which, after expenses, netted $ 3,000. These funds will be quite helpful toward financing my reelection campaign to the N. C. Senate.

Again, Ray, I thank you for your support and friendship. I look forward to continuing to work with you on issues of mutual interest.

With kindest regards and best wishes, I am

Respectfully Yours,

Howard N. Lee

In 1976, Howard Lee ran for Lt. Governor against Lt. Governor Jimmy Green. Howard lost in the primary.

didn't allow black members. On my part, I met with Gregory Poole Jr., owner of MacGregor Downs Country Club, the very next day and we corrected that.

After all that, we appointed builders to the Housing Finance Agency, and they have built thousands of low-income housing units and are still going strong. Today, Raleigh has thousands of low-income apartments and houses. Another thing along these lines: I keep reading about the Republicans' racial gerrymandering of congressional districts. Regardless of what people say, nothing much has changed, whether it be Republican or Democrat. While serving in the legislature, I was on a Democratic committee to redistrict the state. What we did was use the black population to get the most Democrats elected. It was also the Democrats who, in 1991, drew up the new Twelfth District that ran from Durham to Gastonia, creating the "snake district," a 64 percent black majority district that helped elect Mel Watt, a state senator at the time, to the US Congress. By the way, Watt later became chairman of the National Congressional Black Caucus, and in 2013 he became director of the Federal Housing Finance Agency in the Obama administration.

Two of my wife's best friends were Barbara Allen and Jeanette Hyde. They went to lunch or dinner at least once a week for many years. Melba talked to Jeanette every day. These two women were two of the top Democratic women in the state. Barbara was the Democratic state chairperson for over ten years and was involved in almost every Democratic function that took place during her tenure. She was also a vice president of the old Carolina Power and Light Company for many years. Jeanette was appointed ambassador to all of the South Atlantic Islands by President Bill Clinton. Since Jeanette and Jesse Helms lived in the same district and went to the same church, they became good friends, and he took her around to meet all of the other senators in Congress. When Jesse retired from the Senate, he had a retirement party in Raleigh. I was

North Carolina General Assembly
House of Representatives
State Legislative Building
Raleigh 27611

REP. J. RAY SPARROW
62ND DISTRICT - WAKE COUNTY

HOME ADDRESS: 1119 QUEENSFERRY ROAD
CARY, N.C. 27511

OFFICE ADDRESS: STATE LEGISLATIVE BUILDING
ROOM 1315
RALEIGH, N.C. 27611
TELEPHONE: 919/733-5741

COMMITTEES:

LAW ENFORCEMENT, VICE CHAIRMAN
BANKS AND THRIFT INSTITUTIONS
CONSTITUTIONAL AMENDMENTS
CORRECTIONS
FINANCE
HOUSING
JUDICIARY IV
SMALL BUSINESS
TRANSPORTATION

N E W S R E L E A S E

May 2, 1985

Sparrow Works To Simplify Bureaucracy

RALEIGH--Representative Ray Sparrow (D-Wake) has been
working to improve North Carolina's Administrative Procedures
Act--the device through which all the rules and regulations of
state government are created.

"Bureaucrats end up taking over government under the current
system," Sparrow said. "The General Assembly passes legislation
which sets out policies for the state. The bureaucrats then right
the regulations and sometimes these regulations end up being
completely foreign to the original legislative intent--they have
nothing to do with it at all.

"We're trying to get oversight over those rules and
regulations. Right now the same people who put the rules and
regulations together are those an individual would have to appeal
to if he or she didn't happen to like the decision. It ends up
with the rule makers being the accusers, the judges and the
juries and it just isn't right.

"We've had quite a few complaints from the public over
this," Sparrow said.

"Some people have had projects held up for two years for

(more)

page two

no reason except that it takes that long to work through the bureaucratic channels. If it's a business, it can cost millions of dollars unnecessarily," Sparrow said.

"I had some problems with the original legislation because it included licensing boards and other professional oversight groups that I feel do a good job. Now these are exempt from the legislation oversight provisions.

"We've been working to polish this bill for two years. It still isn't finished, but it is well on its way to being good for the people of North Carolina and getting committee approval," Sparrow said.

"The bill is now in the Judiciary IV Committee on which I serve. We've had several public hearings and we've rewritten the bill several times. One of the biggest hurdles to overcome was to make sure that we could meet the requirements of the federal government in assuring that agencies which are given federal jursidiction can meet their duties.

"The bill is about ready for a vote and I think it will be a piece of legislation that will make state government more efficient and more responsive to the needs of the citizens of the state," Sparrow said.

#

Developers laud zone bill passage

By MARY BETH STARR
Staff writer

Local developers are lauding the bill that was passed by the N.C. General Assembly last week allowing for conditional zoning in Cary and Raleigh.

According to the bill, introduced by N.C. Rep. Ray Sparrow of Cary, developers or landowners may submit site plans along with rezoning requests, so the town and neighboring residents would know exactly what was to be built on the land.

Previously, developers could not legally discuss the possible uses for the property when seeking a rezoning due to contract zoning regulations.

Sparrow said the bill has received support from towns all across the state. "We're working on a statewide bill now because we're getting so many requests for it."

"I think it's great," said Dick Ladd, president of Master Real Estate Corporation. "I think that it's going to take a lot of question marks out of developing, and that the governmental authority will be able to see what you're going to do with a piece of property and zone it based on that."

He said it puts pressure on the developer or builder to do what they said they would do with the land. "When the approval and inspections come along, it's got to be what's submitted.

"That's always been an unknown, if we approve this type of zoning, what this guy can put in there. It takes pressure off the town and puts it on the developer."

Russell Buxton of MacGregor Development Co. said, "It's always been difficult to go before the town council and know what you plan to do but not be able to say it.

"Any time that happens, the people who oppose you feel very free to say anything they want to. They usually raise up the most fearful objects."

He said the bill "could have the effect of allowing proponents and opponents of the development to speak on the facts, to deal in reality rather than conjecture."

Buxton said the bill would help developers who want to build an attractive office building, but neighbors fear a junk yard or service station could be put in under the same zoning.

He said the bill "makes a lot of sense."

Don Fraley of The Harlon Group is also pleased with the new bill.

"Our feeling is that it will help speed up the process, and will get the surrounding residents input into the rezoning," he said.

He declined to comment further saying it is just an experimental situation, and he doesn't know how it's going to work in actuality.

According to Glenda Toppe, Cary's planning director, it will be several months before the bill actually goes into effect in Cary.

"We've got to write the ordinance, and it has to go through public hearing.

"We're starting on it just as soon as we can. I hope we could have a public hearing the last meeting in May. But it's going to take some work to get it all in place within the next couple of months."

She said once the public hearing is held, the new ordinance must go to the planning and zoning board, and then on to the Cary Town Council.

The bill allowed the town charter to be changed, but the town is responsible for putting it in the zoning codes.

She said she is not sure if requests that are pending can qualify for the new regulation. Several developers have already asked her if they can be included under the new law. She plans to find out this week what steps they should take.

"I'm pleased it passed," Ms. Toppe said. "I think it's going to help the town out tremendously in rezonings."

Although the time factor will stay the same from the planning staff's viewpoint, she hopes the time spent in review of individual rezonings at public hearings and planning board and council meetings will be reduced.

"We can answer a whole lot more questions for people and work problems out," she said.

invited and accompanied Jeanette to the party, where she made Jesse's retirement speech.

Jeanette; her first husband, Bill Carl; and a partner, James Maynard, started the Golden Corral restaurant chain in 1972. When Bill passed away years later, she met and married Wallace Hyde. Wallace owned an insurance business and a lot of real estate in Asheville. Wallace was also known as one of the most influential politicians in the state, not only in the western part. Wallace and Jeanette bought a big house that looked like a castle on Glenwood Avenue across from the Carolina Country Club. Hardly a week went by that they didn't hold a political fund-raiser or charity event of some sort. They were also good friends with Al Gore and his wife. The Gores dropped by often and stayed there when they were in town. The Hydes would throw parties, and you could expect the governor, past governors, and other important Democrats to be there. I once attended a function there to raise funds to build the Jim Hunt Library at NC State University. The Hydes also had a complex on Key Island in Sarasota, Florida. The complex was huge, with a large separate guest house with a swimming pool between the main house and the guest house. Jeanette stayed there during the winter months. Many other guests from North Carolina, including Melba and I, stayed there often. Wallace passed away several years ago, and Jeannette still goes to Key Island for the winter.

Chapter Six

Walter Davis

WHILE I WAS STILL IN THE LEGISLATURE, around 1984, I was fortunate to meet Walter Davis, a person who has done more in North Carolina politics and for the people of North Carolina than anyone I know. Walter Davis was someone whom very few North Carolinians knew, and he liked to keep it that way. The following is excerpted from his biography, *The Walter Davis Story: One Man Who Made a Difference*, by Ned Cline:

He was one man who made a difference to the politics and people of N.C. He led and lived a fruitful, engaging, and often enigmatic life that produced stories galore. Some are true. Some are not, and many have been embellished with repeated telling through half a century of worthy, albeit most often unorthodox, deeds and achievements.

Davis was booted out of two public high schools as a teenager and barely avoided suspension from military prep school before learning to tow the disciplinary line. He never sat in a college classroom, but he served on the board of trustees of two of the most prestigious universities in the nation at the same time.

Fired from his first two paying jobs, he fled his third following a physical altercation, started at a restaurant, and landed in jail for ninety days for nonpayment of taxes. After this low point, he landed in Midland, TX, where with borrowed money and a used pickup truck he struck it rich in oil transport. He later expanded into oil prospecting, real estate, and other ventures, becoming a multimillionaire.

Davis worked with presidents, kings, senators, governors, and oil field hell raisers, taking the same direct approach with all. He took no grief from any of them. Gruffness, however, was just one side of the man. He also had the heart of a teddy bear and could be as avuncular as anyone when circumstances dictated.

Davis became one of the largest benefactors to the University of North Carolina, plus half a dozen other colleges, and paid all or part of tuition for more than a thousand higher education students. He helped finance two internationally known health service organizations that have made the lives of thousands of people in fifty different countries better.

I consider myself most fortunate to have known Walter Davis. We were very good friends until his death in May 2008. Walter had homes on Bald Head Island and in Chapel Hill, Kill Devil Hills, Midland, Texas, and a suite of rooms at the Governor's Inn near the Research Triangle—all at the same time. He was born and raised near the Outer Banks, and loved that area and the many friends he had there; this was the time in his life when he was spending more time in North Carolina and the suite of rooms where he conducted his business in the Raleigh area. Walter was a registered Republican in Texas, but worked more in the Democratic Party while in North Carolina. George H. W. Bush had a home across the street from Walter's home in Midland, and they were close friends. When Bush was campaigning in North Carolina and called Walter for advice, Walter talked with Bush just like he did with everyone: straight up, with no punches and no happy talk.

Walter Davis was a significant "role player" in the North Carolina political scene for more than thirty years, getting things done without fanfare and mostly by operating behind the scenes. In all the years that I knew Walter Davis, he never sought personal attention or gain, always preferring to remain under the public radar. Davis and I did talk a little politics, but our relationship was more social than anything else. Walter had his own jet plane and crew.

He liked to play gin rummy, and we traveled and played a lot of gin rummy together. He also had a forty-eight-foot boat with a crew on the Outer Banks. His boat captain, Charlie Midgette, was off somewhere all of the time—places like the Gulf of Mexico and the Caribbean, entertaining people who Walter wanted to entertain—John Connally, Luther Hodges, Herbert Bonner, Carl Albert, Lyndon Johnson, and Terry Sanford, to name a few. As I said earlier, Davis's base of operations during the legislative session was the Radisson Governor's Inn, a hotel in the Research Triangle Park. Davis used the hotel suite as his headquarters for more than twenty-five years. It would not be an exaggeration to say that as many legislative policies were decided at the Radisson Governor's Inn as in the halls of the Legislative Building. I was there many times playing gin rummy when legislators and many other important people came to see Walter. I also was with Walter the day UNC named a library after him.

A caricature of Walter Davis drawn by Charlotte cartoonist Eugene Payne at the suggestion of Davis's friend Skipper Bowles. Bowles said the references to oil wells, fishing, gin rummy, and good times reflected the business and social aspects of Davis's life.

Bald Head Island Lighthouse

I was with Walter also when he sold Bald Head Island to George Mitchell, another Texas oil millionaire. Walter had a business partner named Jim Harrington who looked after all of his real estate deals. Walter would buy them and Jim would handle the details. Jim was a prominent Republican and once the CEO of Pinehurst Golf and Country Club. He also served as head of the Department of Transportation under Governor Jim Martin. Jim Harrington and I were the best of friends. Like many of my closest friends and associates, I was once his company commander in the National Guard. Walter Davis and Jim Harrington developed the first planned unit development (PUD) in Cary, among many other real estate projects. Jim still lives on Bald Head Island.

Walter and our wives shared many good times together as well. One of the best trips we ever took was up to a cabin he owned on Canada's Great Bear Lake in the Arctic Circle. The lake is one of the best trophy fishing spots in the world. We spent two weeks up there fishing and playing a few hours of gin rummy while our wives played bridge and took in the scenery. The only way you can get to the lake is by float plane, as there are no roads in that part of the Northwest Territories. The lake is frozen ten months of the year and the sun never fully goes down.

My wife Melba and I and two other couples—Dr. Richard Saleeby and his wife Doris, and Joe Lee Jr. and his wife Ruth Johnson—spent a

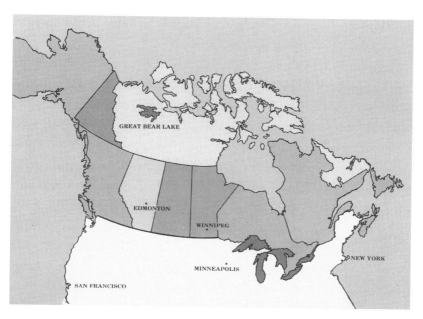

Arctic Circle Lodge on Canada's Great Bear Lake

lot of time with the Davises, traveling and just hanging out together. Dr. Saleeby had a practice in Raleigh and knew almost everyone in Wake County. Joe ran Johnson's Jewelers, a company founded by Ruth's parents in 1929 and still a thriving business today.

A couple of times a year, the Davises would host a party at their home in The Oaks near Chapel Hill Country Club. Most all of the guests were people associated with the University of North Carolina at Chapel Hill. The UNC Board of Trustees, most of the sports coaches, and many other UNC staff would be there. I recall my wife Melba would always engage in a conversation with basketball coach Dean Smith, trying to lure him away to coach the NC State Wolfpack team. He would always humor her and then politely turn her down. As a lifetime Wolfpacker, I always felt a little out of place at those events, but the Tar Heels were always nice to me, and we were mostly on a first-name basis.

Keeping Walter on schedule and taking care of his needs was more than a full-time job for JoAnn, and she also had to take care of their family and social needs. But she was always friendly, and looked happy.

I could tell a million stories about Walter. One that really stands out in my mind has to do with how much he loved Orange Crush soda. He appeared on the Kitty Hawk Pier very early one morning in 1968 to buy a bottle of Orange Crush soda to quench his thirst after a night of card playing at the Elks Club in Elizabeth City. When the owner told him he didn't carry Orange Crush soda, Davis said something like he "ought to." The owner came back at Davis in something less than a polite tone, saying if Davis didn't like the way the pier was operated, he should buy it and run it his way. Davis said, "Fine," he would do just that. And so he did, purchasing it on the spot for ninety-six thousand dollars, the amount asked for; then he immediately directed the man, who now worked for him, to order an ample supply of Orange Crush. I drank a few Orange Crush sodas with Walter on that pier.

You may remember that actor Andy Griffith retired and lived in

Manteo. Walter and Andy were the best of friends. According to Ned Cline, "Griffith tells one story that describes Davis's benevolence to people he had never met. 'The wife of a friend of mine, whom Walter didn't even know, was suffering from a terminal disease following treatment in Houston, Texas, and couldn't fly home commercially,' Griffith said. 'Walter heard about her situation. He sent his plane across the country to bring her home to North Carolina. I sent him a check for the cost of the trip, but he wouldn't accept payment. He sent my check back. That's just the way he was. He was one of the most generous people I have ever known and did do much good for so many for so long. He was a fine man and a fine friend.'"

Cline describes "Davis's early introduction in the middle 1980s to state senator Mark Basnight of Manteo, the man many political insiders now perceive as perhaps the most powerful elected officeholder in North Carolina. Davis took an immediate liking to the normally soft-spoken and then relatively young Basnight, first as a building contractor willing to listen and later as a political candidate willing to learn." I like to say that Walter Davis "raised" Marc Basnight, who went on to become a senator serving in the legislature for nine terms and almost twenty-five years. Some politicians today still complain about all the state funds that went to the Outer Banks and Eastern North Carolina while Basnight was in charge of the legislature.

"MONK" HARRINGTON AND "PIG" PARKER

Two other men who were good friends of mine and Walter Davis's were J.J. "Monk" Harrington and Don L. "Pig" Parker. Harrington served in the legislature as a senator for twenty-eight years, his last four as pro tempore. He owned an agricultural equipment company in Lewiston that was a mainstay of the local economy. Pig Parker owned a bank in Colerain, also in Bertie County, and was on the North Carolina Agriculture Commission for over twenty years. He called himself a peanut farmer, but Pig, a good friend of Commissioner Jim Graham's, had more political power than most could wish for or imagine. Everybody east of Raleigh knew not to attempt to run for political office "down East" unless you first touched base with Pig.

If you were a male Democrat serving in the legislature during those years, you were always invited to a deer hunt at Monk Harrington's farm in Bertie County. Pig, a close friend of Monk's, made all of the arrangements, assigning people to stay in one of Monk's houses on his farm. It was a two-day hunt, and the first night on Friday there would be around ten bonfires with politicians gathered around them, talking politics. One particular thing I remember is that most of the legislators, governors, and past governors, and all of the sheriffs from Eastern North Carolina were there. There were probably more bills passed that weekend than the rest of the legislative session. I was lucky enough to stay in one of the houses on Monk's farm. It so happens that Marc Basnight, who was on the Highway Commission at that time, and Tom Bradshaw were staying in the same house and we played a little poker that night. There had been about five hundred politicians standing around the bonfires that night, but when we got up to hunt around six o'clock in the morning, only about ten of us showed up.

Monk Harrington and I got to be really good friends. He ran several farms and also built manufactured low-income housing. I would advise him on the manufactured houses, and sometimes, when he stayed in Raleigh on weekends, we would play golf at MacGregor Downs Country Club. Pig Parker's family and mine also became very close. We stayed many times on his farm in Bertie County, and also in his beach house on Ocracoke Island. Pig and his wife, Bolton, are both deceased now, but we stay in touch with their daughter, Janette, who lives on Wrightsville Beach.

Chapter Seven

My Run for the Senate

IN 1987, WHEN I WAS FINISHING UP my term in the House, Liston Ramsey was also finishing his eight-year term as Speaker of the House, having served forty years in the North Carolina House of Representatives. As my term was ending, Wilma Woodard decided not to run for the state senate. At that time, three senators were representing Wake, Lee, and Harnett Counties. The other two senators, Joe Johnson and Bill Stanton, asked me to run for Wilma's Fourteenth District seat. After much research and deliberation, I decided to run. My Democratic primary opponent was J.K. Sherron, who was very active in the Democratic Party. J.K. was working for the Department of Administration, and he also had a partnership in a real estate business. J.K. and I had been friends for years. We'd gone to NC State about the same time, and we'd also worked in many Democratic campaigns together. As a matter of fact, he got his state job after working in the Jim Hunt campaign. J.K. was raised in Harnett County and had many friends and family in that part of the state.

I figured this was going to be a tough battle, and I was right. I worked almost full-time, campaigning for four months from morning to late at night. Every week, I would spend half a day in Wake County, half a day in Lee County, then a full day in Harnett County. Harnett County was a strange place to campaign. The county is divided into two parts by the Cape Fear River, and the two parts are like two separate worlds. The sheriff pretty much ran Harnett County, and I was told I'd better get his okay before I did anything. The sheriff's race is the main political race in every election in Harnett County. The people who live on the Dunn side of the river line up against the people on the Lillington side of the river, vying for the winner in the sheriff's race. Whoever was elected would fire all the deputies of the defeated sheriff's and hire new ones. I read in the newspaper recently that they still had some of the same problems in recent elections, which reminds me of something that happened when I was working in the Muskie campaign for Governor Scott. I asked Scott for a list of his key people in each of the hundred counties in North Carolina. Would you believe that ninety were sheriffs? Interestingly, in some counties in North Carolina today, the sheriffs are apparently still running things.

But, back to my run for the senate. In Harnett County, you had to buy votes, something that happened over most of the county. For instance, in one town there was a precinct chairman who controlled 130 votes. A candidate would pay her five hundred dollars and she would deliver 130 votes. Most precincts were the same way. I knew a lot of people in Harnett County because of my association with the Jaycees, the Homebuilders, and the National Guard armory we had built in Dunn, but I was still at a disadvantage, because I didn't believe in buying votes.

The day before the election, a lawyer friend called me up and said that I'd better have someone down at a particular polling place in Harnett County before nine o'clock in the morning. I asked why, and he said, "The voting machines will break down and they'll bring in wooden voter boxes that already have ballots in them." I sent one of my campaign workers to check it out, and sure enough, the machines "broke down" and they brought in wooden voter boxes. As you can imagine, we didn't get much help from the sheriff, who stood by idly. But even worse than that, the day before the election, my wife, who'd just come home from the post office, asked me to come out to look at something in the trunk of her car. She opened the trunk, and there were over twelve thousand pieces of returned mail. At that time, you could buy mailing labels from any county Democratic headquarters, and we had bought the Harnett County labels from the Wake County Democratic Headquarters. Would you believe that all of the Harnett County mailing labels we brought from the Wake County headquarters were for deceased folks or people who had moved away? We were stunned. Out of thirty-five thousand votes, you would think that we might've gotten enough if we had been given an accurate mailing list. But no, we lost the election by only eighty-two votes! It was enough to make you cry. They say that, at the time, it was the most expensive state senate race ever in North Carolina. Shortly after my loss, I went to see Lieutenant Governor Bob Jordan, who was also head of the state Democratic Party, and told him that I was thinking about going to the *News & Observer*. Bob was a good friend and I had worked in his campaign, but he talked me out of going to the papers because he said it would hurt the Democratic Party badly. So much for old-school Democrats. Incidentally, Bob Jordan's administrative assistant at that time was Lois Brown. Lois and her husband, Bill, were very close friends of ours. Later Lois and my wife, Melba, were in business together.

Incidentally, we knew who sold us the bogus list of voters. This person was a longtime Democrat and held a high office in the party. I decided then it would not change my life and still feel the same now. If that person can live with what he did, that's his problem.

Losing the election by only eighty-two votes was particularly hurtful, especially since I didn't get as much of the black vote as I felt I should've gotten. I knew that they didn't like my vote against the Greensboro bill, but I had worked for many black candidates over the years. Some of the things I did over the years on black issues are as follows:

Bob Jordan, lt. governor and good friend

+ Worked on fund-raisers for Saint Augustine's College
+ Worked on fund-raisers for Shaw University
+ Helped raise funds to build a YMCA in Southeast Raleigh at the urging of black community leaders
+ Was chairman of Raleigh's Downtown Housing Corporation, which built low-income housing in Southeast Raleigh
+ As a contractor, remodeled and added to many black churches
+ Built the residence for the black funeral home owner in Apex
+ Employed from fifteen to thirty black employees in my construction business for about fifty years
+ Joined the Southern Christian Leadership Conference, ten-year member
+ Worked on state government jobs and appointments for many blacks

+ Worked on the United Negro College Fund
+ Worked on the campaigns of many black candidates, including Mayor Howard Lee, Representative Dan Blue, Senator John Winters, Mayor Clarence Lightner (first black mayor of Raleigh), Sheriff John Baker (first black sheriff of Wake County), and Ken Wilkins, a prominent black candidate for the House.

When J.K. and I went before the black caucus in Southeast Raleigh, one question they asked me was, when a black bill comes up in the legislature, will you support it? My answer was, "Yes, if it is a good bill." J.K. Sherron's answer was, "Just tell me what you want and I will support it." Maybe the blacks thought I didn't do enough for them.

Regardless of my disappointment, as you now know, I stuck around and supported several more Democratic candidates for a few more years—Jim Hunt in his race against Jesse Helms in 1990. I must say, I think Jim Hunt, a moderate Democrat, was one of the best governors we ever had, which reminds me.... When I was a young man in the Jaycees, I met Jim Gardner at a Jaycee function in Rocky Mount. We were all sitting at a table drinking beer, and Jim and his partner had just started the Hardee's restaurant chain. During the conversation, Jim said that he planned to run for governor someday. Well, he did run, but Jim Hunt beat him in a landslide.

Many people are under the impression that Jim Gardner started Hardee's restaurants. Wilbut Hardee admantly denies that Gardner had anything to do with building the first Hardee's. Jim Gardner and Leonard Rawls did join Wilbur to launch franchises of some 3,600 Hardee's restaurants.

Jim Gardner was strongly involved in North Carolina politics and in many business ventures across the nation. Some say he was a great salesman but a poor manager. Gardner was a very colorful personality.

Grady Jefferys and Charles Heatherly wrote a book titled *Jim Gardner: A Question of Character* that is an interesting read.

I want to mention another longtime Democratic friend here: Fred Morrison. When I was campaigning with Fred Morrison, he knew almost every Jaycee in the state. Even though that was about sixty years ago, he still keeps up with every one of them, including me. Fred also worked

Fred Morrison

with me on the Governor Scott campaign. He was the legal aide for Governor Scott and is still serving as an administrative law judge. Fred was recently honored with the first Administrative Law Award for Excellence from the North Carolina Bar Association. Even though he is a big-time Democrat, we are still good friends.

At one time, the Jaycees were very much involved in the North Carolina political system. I had the privilege of working with a number of Jaycees over the years: Governor Bob Scott, Haw River; Fred Morrison was a past state Jaycee president and is now a state law judge; Frank Daniels Jr.'s family owned the Raleigh *News & Observer*; Howard Twiggs of Raleigh served several terms in the state legislature and was past president of the North Carolina Academy of Trial Lawyers as well as the Association of Trial Lawyers of America; Tom Bradshaw served as mayor of both Raleigh and Bald Head Island; Lucius Jones served as mayor of Wendell; Paul Pulley from Durham served in the state legislature; John Alexander Jr. from Raleigh is now serving in the state legislature; Bob Cossell served on the Cary Town Council; Al Adams from Raleigh served many years in the state legislature; Irvin

Aldridge from Mebane served as state Jaycee president and as secretary of the Department of Local Affairs; Oscar Harris from Dunn served in the state legislature; Melba Sparrow served as secretary for the Raleigh Jaycees and later as the first woman on the Cary Town Council; Joe Johnson from Raleigh served many years in the state legislature; Charles Scott from Cary served as the North Carolina Adjutant General; Jim Melvin served many years as mayor of Greensboro; Larry Jordan served as mayor of Apex an also served in the state legislature; Sam Johnson of Raleigh served in the State House; George Little from Southern Pines served as an aide to Governor Jim Holshouser; Holshouser was a Boone Jaycee; Zander Guy was mayor of Jacksonville; Bob Wynn from Raleigh served in the state senate; Bob Mathery served as mayor of Zebulon; Buddie Gettys served as mayor of Spencer; Bill McDonald served as state Jaycee president and mayor of Hickory; Cubby Wilson served as mayor of Lumberton; Chuck Flack served as mayor of Boone; Luther Britt of Lumberton served in the state senate; Jollin Beck served as mayor of Elizabeth City; John Hatcher of Winston Salem served as Governor Dan Moore's military aide; Jim Gardner of Rocky Mount served both in congress and as Lieutenant Governor of North Carolina; Peggy Stamey, whose husband Jim was a very active Democrat and a Cary Jaycee, served ten years in the legislature; Dr. Tom Brooks served several terms on the Cary Town Council; Dr. Ed Davis Harold Ritter, and Fred Bond all served as mayors of Cary; Ed Owens of Cary served many years as head of the Raleigh Building Department; Bob Farmer of Raleigh served in the legislature; Marvin Koonce, president of the Raleigh Jaycees, worked in many capacities at the national Jaycees level and his wife served many terms on the Wake County School Board; Casper Holroyd from Raleigh served in the legislature; Buck Bunn from Raleigh served in the legislature; Burley Mitchell from Raleigh was the Chief Justice of North Carolina from the early 1950s through the 1980s. There were over two hundred Jaycee chapters throughout the state, with many of those having more than two hundred members. The Jaycees were one of the largest associations in the nation. At that time it was an all-male club of strictly young men due to the maximum age limit of thirty-five. It goes without saying that the Jaycees had a major impact on state and local politics. Today it is hard to find a Jaycee chapter in North Carolina. Young men's priorities have changed. I think the Rotary Clubs much replaced the Jaycees. These are just some of the Jaycees I worked with over the years. I'm sure I have left out many others. I believe there were many Jaycees who served on virtually every city and town council all across the state.

Today, the Democratic Party keeps going to the left, until now it is pretty much a socialist party. Moderates like me have been leaving the party since the early fifties. In 2000 I switched to the Republican Party, but in recent years I have become "unaffiliated." In the past I have supported Republicans—Richard Vinroot for governor, Senator Tamara

*Jack Hawke and Ray Sparrow. Jack was very involved in the Republican
Party for many years and served as chairman at one time.*

*Ray and Melba Sparrow, gubernatorial candidate Richard Vinroot,
Ann and Jim Harrington at a fundraiser for Vinroot held at our house*

Barringer, Paul Stam, John Alexander Jr., Gary Pendleton, Governor Pat
McCrory, and Nelson Dollar, to name a few. John Alexander's father was
a lifelong Democrat, and I worked in many campaigns with John Sr. Vinroot was the mayor of Charlotte. I liked Richard and think he would have
made a great governor. The only thing he had against him, in my opinion,
was that he played basketball for UNC. I think that Senator Barringer is
an outstanding state senator and would make a great governor.

North Carolina General Assembly
Senate Chamber
State Legislative Building
Raleigh 27611

SENATOR BOB JORDAN
HOME ADDRESS: P. O. BOX 98
MOUNT GILEAD, N. C. 27306

July 20, 1983

The Honorable Ray Sparrow
North Carolina General Assembly
State Legislative Building - Room 633
Raleigh, North Carolina 27611

Dear Ray:

Just a note to wish you a few days of peace and quiet
you well deserve after these last few weeks of this
difficult session.

You can be proud of the part you have played in seeing
that this legislature has faced up to its responsibility
of addressing the problems of the people, and of seeing
that North Carolina continues to move forward. There
have been no easy answers nor perfect solutions, but you
have made the tough decisions that were necessary.

I have enjoyed serving with you, and look forward to that
continued opportunity in the future.

Sincerely,

Bob Jordan

BJ:rh

Ray! you'll be a real asset to this legislature. I look forward to working with you here and on the campaign. Friend, Bob

ANSON MONTGOMERY RICHMOND SCOTLAND STANLY UNION
17TH DISTRICT
NOT PAID FOR AT STATE EXPENSE

April 29, 1986

Dear Fellow Voters:

My Name is Ed Carson, and I am supporting Ray Sparrow, a two-term State Representative, for a seat in the N.C. State Senate because Ray Sparrow supported our community when we needed it.

1. As a member and as a chairman of the Raleigh Downtown Housing Improvement Corporation, Ray Sparrow worked hard to provide low and moderate income housing for the people of the South-East Raleigh.

2. As a member of Governor Jim Hunt's advisory staff, Ray Sparrow also worked with the Governor and the legislature in setting up and promoting the N.C. Housing Finance Agency, an agency that has provided many thousands of low and moderate homes for all North Carolinians.

3. When the need for financial assistance struck our community, Ray Sparrow was there. Ray Sparrow was with us in raising money for St. Augustine College, Shaw University, The Garner Road Y.M.C.A., Estey Hall and many other projects in our community.

4. In our struggle to gain political representation by black office holders, Ray Sparrow was there, working hard for our candidates, both financially and physically. Ray Sparrow openly supported Wake Sheriff John Baker, N.C. State Senator John W. Winters, Representative Dan Blue, Commissioner Elizabeth Cofield, and others.

5. On the floor of the N.C. House of Representatives, Ray Sparrow was there when we needed him. Ray Sparrow stood up to be counted, as a man who believes in "Affirmative Actions", and "Equal Rights" for all people. Ray Sparrow supported and voted in the "Affirmative" for legislation dear to our hearts, such as, the Doctor Martin Luther King Recognition Day for North Carolina, goals for minority business set asides, appointing of minority as pages in the State House, and many others.

Let us not forget Ray Sparrow on Election Day, May 6, 1986.

Ray Sparrow has a track record that is second to none of the other senatorial candidates. I invite you to compare it to the other seven senatorial candidates, and you will find that not one of them has a record that reflects the friend that we have in Ray Sparrow.

Let us keep this friend working for us, as your Senator for the N.C. 14th Senatorial District. We must not forget those who stood with us when we needed a friend. You will be able to vote for three senatorial candidates to serve you in the N.C. State Senate. Please be sure that Ray Sparrow gets one of your three votes.

Vote for Ray Sparrow on May 6, to be your N.C. State Senator.

Many thanks to all of you.

Sincerely,

ED CARSON

Ed Carson

Endorsement from Ed Carson, up and coming black leader
and member of the Raleigh Chamber of Commerce

P.O. BOX 328
RALEIGH, NORTH CAROLINA 27602

December 16, 1981

Mr. Ray Sparrow
1119 Queensferry Road
Cary, North Carolina 27511

Dear Ray:

I want to again express my deepest gratitude to you for serving as
a host at the Reception held on December 2, at Mission Valley in
my honor.

I was extremely pleased with the turnout and feel the evening was
enjoyed by all who attended. It was a successful and gratifying
evening in that we managed to "fatten the war chest" dollarwise;
and the words of commitment and support were most encouraging.

I am proud to have the loyal support of such influential, concerned,
progressive leaders and men of integrity and honor as you. I shall
always do my best to ensure the faith you have placed in me remains
so earned. I pledge to continue to do all within my power to make
the Wake County Sheriff's Department Number 1 in the State ... providing the services and meeting the needs of the citizens of our
fine county.

With warmest personal regards, I remain

Most Sincerely,

John H. Baker, Jr.

John Baker was the first black sheriff in Wake County

North Carolina General Assembly
Senate Chamber
State Legislative Building
Raleigh 27611

March 4, 1991

Mr. Ray Sparrow, President
Sparrow Construction Co., Inc.
P. O. Box 33609
Raleigh, North Carolina 27636

Dear Ray:

Thank you for your kind note of congratulations. The decision to move to the Senate and the resulting transition have been difficult. However, I think the move will be best for my constituents and for me in the long run.

I was proud to support your candidacy for the Board of Governors. Although you didn't win this time, I hope you'll try it again. There was a great field this time.

Please let me know how I can help in the Senate.

With kind regards, I am

Very truly yours,

Roy A. Cooper, III

RAC/sm

I was friends with Roy Cooper, current governor of North Carolina, when he was in the State House.

Chapter Eight

Summing Up My Old-School Political Life

YOU MAY HAVE DETECTED from some of my remarks that I'm not ready to give up all of my old-school ways as far as my politics go. Some of the things that are going on today in Republican-controlled national politics as well as Republican-controlled statewide politics really gall me. Our current president is a Republican and has a Republican Congress, yet he has not gotten any of his campaign promises legislated through Congress, nor has he behaved at all times in a manner befitting a president of the United States. On the statewide level, the situation is even worse. We have a Democratic governor and a Republican-controlled legislature that is constantly trying to shove everything the governor stands for down his throat. They even stooped to passing legislation to limit his power shortly before the governor was sworn in. In addition, the legislature seems hell-bent on fighting every bill, even the good bills.

I have two very good friends with whom I played golf for over thirty years. They are also the best of friends until they try to discuss politics. One of them is a retired college professor and the other a retired computer expert. The retired professor thinks the Democratic Party can do no wrong and the computer expert thinks that Donald Trump hung the moon. When the two of them get together, it is a knock-down, all-out confrontation.

Both of these gentlemen are as bright and well-educated and as nice as any men you would ever want to meet. However, when it comes to politics, they only have mouths—their ears disappear. If two best friends can't have a civil, friendly conversation on politics, how do we ever expect our two main political parties, which now despise each other, to ever work with each other?

Some of the giants of the old-school politics were Thad Eure Sr., who was the secretary of state for fifty years; Jim Graham, who was the agriculture commissioner for forty years; and state treasurers Edwin Gill and Harlan Bowles, who were keepers of the public purse for a total of fifty years. These folks presided over a historic comeback for North Carolina after its precipitous fall during the Great Depression, in which North Carolina saw more local governments in default than any other state. Out of chaos came the best-managed state and local government story in the United States, which is the basis for our continuing Triple-A credit rating.

I spent several years on the North Carolina Alternative Energy Commission. We not only promoted solar and wind alternative energy but spent a lot of time improving ways to save energy in homes and office buildings. I believe the commission saved millions of dollars in new and old buildings. In addition, Tom Bradshaw and I were owners of a solar energy company. We made trips out west to Phoenix, Arizona, and Albuquerque, New Mexico, looking at solar plants and buildings. In the western parts of the United States about 80 percent of all housing and most commercial buildings have some kind of solar system. Out west, they have about 80 percent sunlight during the day, whereas North Carolina has only about 50 percent sunlight during the day.

I also helped start the Solar Experimental House at NC State College, now NC State University. It is still in operation today. Our construction company also built Sun Ridge, the first solar subdivision in Wake County. Sun Ridge has about thirty attached units with all solar features, including extra insulation, insulated glass with most of the glass on the sunny side, thicker walls, the most efficient HVAC units made, and a rooftop solar panel attached to the water heater.

Recently, a good bill came before the legislature advocating a wind farm spreading 104 massive turbines over twenty-two thousand acres of farmland in Pasquotank and Perquimans County, generating enough energy to power sixty-one thousand homes a year. Despite recent efforts by legislative leaders to kill the bill, the $400 million project, North Carolina's first wind farm, began full operation in February. Senate president pro tem Phil Berger and House Speaker Tim Moore tried to kill it, raising phony objections about the turbines interfering with military radar, despite the navy saying there was no problem. The *News & Observer* wrote, "What their opposition was really about was serving the interests of the fossil fuel industry at the expense of renewable resources." Whether that was their reasoning or not, it was a good bill and they should not have opposed it. Thankfully, some elected officials in our legislature still can recognize a good bill and vote for it despite partisan politics.

Chapter Nine

A Little More on the Dark Side

JUST A LITTLE MORE ON THE DARK SIDE of the Democratic Party in the late 1950s. Zeno Ponder, who ruled mountainous Madison County, was indicted on federal charges related to the sale of land he owned that was in the path of a state highway. He was a key Hunt ally. State AFL-CIO president Wilbur Hobby went to jail for misusing $1 million in job-training funds. He was a key Hunt ally. By 1999, a third legislative machine arose, headed by Jim Black. He was elected to four terms as Speaker of the House. A key ally of Democratic governor Jim Hunt and Mike Easley, Black's aggressive fund-raising landed him in prison. Others who went astray of the law were Michael Decker, a Republican, who switched to the Democratic Party and went to prison for accepting a fifty-thousand-dollar bribe for switching his vote to Democratic Speaker Jim Black. Representative Frank Balance went to jail for misuse of state funds. These are just the ones we know about.

The decline of the old-fashioned political machines means that candidates can no longer count on political bosses to deliver the vote for them, which means candidates often have to raise large amounts of political money to make their case to voters. In my opinion, that's why most politicians today are *owned* by someone—mostly big businesses.

Cash in brown paper bags is no longer passed and winked at, but money is available to buy votes in places you wouldn't dream of. North Carolina remains culturally conservative, more like Alabama than California. I read somewhere that North Carolina is a state "caught between the memories of the past and its dreams of the future." I agree. The Democratic Party is not the same party today as when I was serving in the legislature in the middle 1980s. By the way, I almost forgot that I ran for office one more time before I decided that I would retire from politics.

J .K. Sherron, who beat me for Wake County Senate by eighty-two votes out of thirty-five thousand, only served two terms. So I decided I would give it one last try in 1992. I ran against Linda Gunter, a Cary schoolteacher who taught civics in Cary High School for over twenty years. She was well-liked in Cary and had worked in the Democratic Party most of her life. When I was in the legislature, I was invited to speak to her classes several times, so we were friends. Running against Linda Gunter was not a good decision. It was at a time when the Democratic Party had gone full circle; everything was identity politics, and to run against a woman schoolteacher was political suicide. I lost, of course, and Linda went on to beat a Republican named Paul "Skip" Stam. Linda served only one term, spending most of her time teaching school. She was always escorting five or six high school students around the Legislative Building. She lost the next election to a Republican named John Carrington. Skip Stam, from Apex, went on to beat Bill Freeman for a seat in the House, even though he lost one term to Larry Jordan. Stam served sixteen years in the House and was very successful, ending up as Speaker pro tempore.

A typical example of how much the Democratic Party had changed by the early 1990s took place when I ran against Linda Gunter. For years I had worked for various women's issues and women candidates. One I remember was Peggy Stamey. Peggy served in the House for almost ten years. She and her husband, Jim, were good friends of ours. Jim and I were in the Cary Jaycees, and we worked on many Democratic campaigns together. I served as campaign chairman for two of Peggy's campaigns, and she won both of them. A few years later she told some friends that she thought I was mad at her because she told me that she had to vote for Linda Gunter because Linda was a woman. Several other women told me the same thing, even though I had worked in their campaigns or helped them get jobs. The Democratic Party, by this time, had gone totally for identity politics. I was not mad at Peggy then, and I'm not mad at anybody now. Life's too short to hold grudges. I did help get Peggy a full-time job with the state Prisons Commission.

This reminds me of another funny story while I was out on the campaign trail. One Saturday while I was campaigning in the town of Apex, I met a group of about twenty people carrying signs and yelling, "Close Down Shearon Harris Nuclear Power Plant!" They asked me what I was campaigning for, and I told them I was running for state senate in Wake County. They wanted to know if I would vote to close down Shearon Harris. I said, "Absolutely not!" I knew I wouldn't get their vote because they said they had talked to Senator Joe Johnson earlier in the day and he'd said he would vote to close it down. When I got home that night, I could hardly wait to call Joe Johnson, one of three senators from Wake County. Bill Staton was the other one. Joe was a lawyer, and I knew that he did some legal work for CP&L, which owned the power plant at that time. I said, "Joe, you didn't really tell those demonstrators that you would vote to close down the nuclear plant, did you?"

He said, "Ray, you will never make it in politics. I told them that if you and Bill Staton would, then they could count on me."

"Joe, you know Bill and I would never vote to close the plant," I said.

"Yes, I know," said Joe. "So I told them the truth, didn't I?"

Chapter Ten

Final Thoughts

30 PERCENT OF REGISTERED VOTERS today are "unaffiliated," which means that neither the Democratic nor the Republican Party could win an election without their vote. That is more than 2 million unaffiliated registered voters in North Carolina, and this percentage of voters is growing bigger each election. I believe that in the near future they will form a new party and will control the elections in North Carolina and the United States.

At present, I think that North Carolina is still a God-fearing, gun-owning, lock-'em-up-and-throw-away-the-key, pro-military state. Some have said that we are a state that loves NASCAR, pickup trucks, and plainspoken politicians who don't put on many airs. As for race relations and controversies, I think race will always be a determining factor in North Carolina politics. In the early 1900s, North Carolina was a blue state, but in the early 1950s the state had turned purple. But the 2016 statewide election showed signs that the Democrats are beginning to move further to the left. If something doesn't change in the next ten years, I believe we will become a red state. Looking at the 2016 national election, the nation has definitely gone red. With a new Democratic Party leader who some say has strong socialist leanings, and no strong future leaders in sight, it looks as if the party will have problems in the future. Further, the Democratic Party today relies too heavily on identity politics. They're all about labor unions, teachers' unions, lawyers' unions, gays, lesbians, transgenders, and women's libbers. They don't seem to care about the middle class and the working class anymore.

The goal of the modern Democratic Party is to maximize the number of Americans who believe they are totally dependent on politics for some key zone in life—their retirement income, children's education, health care, parents' health care, housing, food stamps, or even their employment. The greater number of dependent Americans who need aid and see the government as their parent, the stronger the left gets.

Democrats and the media care more about the advancement of their cause than Republicans care about preserving the Constitution.

One big misconception is that the Republicans are the party of Wall Street. Actually Wall Street has given ten times the amount of money to the Democratic Party than the Republican Party, and there are more billionaire Democrats than Republicans. Once one realizes that big government works for Wall Street bankers who float all bonds that underwrite government spending, then the picture becomes clear.

As a longtime Democrat, I have often been puzzled by the relationship between blacks and the Democratic Party. At each election period the Democratic Party starts yelling about racism, and yet for the past sixty years of black support for the Democratic Party, black society has gone downhill every year, except for a few black politicians who are given political jobs or money. The black community is in the worst shape it has ever been. Their family structure is gone, their employment is gone, and they are killing each other at a high rate. Once the Democrats are elected, you hear no more about the black problem until the next election.

I read the comments about draining the swamp in Washington, but I think we could start closer to home and look at draining the swamp in Raleigh as well. I think that most people who are elected in North Carolina are sincere and honest about doing the right thing. But after being serenaded and complimented in office during their first term, the only thing they are interested in is reelection. By then, most of them will have been bought out by lobbyists, special-interest groups, big business, or people with more money than you can shake a stick at. I am talking about both parties, not just the Democrats. So what can we do about it? I think it would help to limit the terms of office to a maximum of twelve years, and limit being a lobbyist after they get out of office to a maximum of five years.

I believe that limiting all elective offices from courthouse to the White House, would encourage more people to get involved in our political system bringing fresh ideas to the table, and would eliminate the problem of lifetime, bought politicians. Such limits should apply to school boards, city and county commissions, and even committees of all government boards. Without them, individuals become entrenched and set in their ways, unable to think outside the box.

One of the biggest problems today is the size of our government. We must, somehow, cut the size of government. Every time we have an election, we appoint new chairs of this or that department. These people

The big difference between the Democratic Party and the Republican Party is: the Democratic Party likes to use government regulations to control the people and the Republican Party wants government out of the way!

hardly have time to find where their offices are before the next election. Meanwhile, the government employees keep on making new rules and regulations that pile up year after year. The government employees run this nation, not the politicians.

The average voter hasn't the foggiest idea of how our political system works. They think you elect a party or a candidate and those individuals try to implement the platform on which they campaigned. However, that is not what really happens. The parties and the candidates don't run government; the bureaucrats do. The parties and the candidates are often only in office one or two terms while the government employees are there sometimes as long as fifty years or more. They decide whether or not a law is implemented. Unfortunately, most of these people belong to one party or the other, and if they don't like a law, they will not implement it, and there is nothing we can do about it. It is practically impossible to fire a government employee, no matter how bad they are. When the Democratic Party wins, the government turns a little more socialistic. When the Republicans win, the government stays about the same. Until we can find a way to get rid of state and federal employees who won't to do their jobs—and there are millions—our government will never be any better.

Now I know that President Trump is not perfect even though he thinks he is. Even though the liberal news media might not get him impeached, it's not going to matter because few, if any, of his programs will be implemented because of the liberal government employees.

Unfortunately, the Democratic Party believes that by pumping money into social programs, they will solve the low-income problems. I know that most Democrats are sincere about this, but study after study shows just the opposite effect. When you strap more regulations on and raise taxes to pay for these things, then the price of goods goes up. Even though the middle-income people can now pay for things, the poor can't afford to pay the higher prices. Instead, they have to cut out food, heat, or rent. They can't even think about health care! Some government programs are a must, but when we cut out foreign goods that are cheaper, it just makes it harder on poor folks. More government spending is not the answer.

I know that many businesses give a lot to charities, but we need to encourage them to double their contributions to help the poor. The future of America lies in the hands of millennials. There are no more Jaycees and Tom Bradshaws to save us. Yes, children are growing up in a tech-savvy society where hard work and grit are all but forgotten. Our children are coddled so much that they can't even communicate without technology. I have heard stories of parents doing their children's homework so that the child can have more time for social interaction and playing computer games. This is a terrible disservice that will leave our children ill prepared for the real world. Are we raising a generation of me-first young people who don't even recognize poverty when they see it?

The future of our country lies in the hands of the millennials. I have to wonder about some of our college professors who incite young people to rally and destroy property. If we can't count on our educators to teach civility to our young people, who can we count on?

If you have children or grandchildren still in school I strongly recommend you read a book titled *Old School* by Bill O'Reilly. The book describes the difference between life thirty to forty years ago and what he calls the "snowflake" society of today.

Our nation is in big trouble, and if something isn't done about it soon, we are not going to be a world power much longer.

Ever year Chapman University conducts a survey across the nation to find out what Americans fear most. It wasn't terrorism, financial meltdown, climate change, losing a loved one, going broke, or another war. The number-one fear for Americans in 2016, by a margin of almost 20 percent, was corrupt government officials.

By Election Day 2016, we'd become a nation where large parts of the country no longer trusted Washington or the news media and had grown tired and suspicious of Friday afternoon document dumps, where the hope seemed to be that the latest unseemly news stories would get buried by sports stories over the weekend.

Large parts of the country had grown tired of sending politicians to Washington, where they didn't do what they'd promised and yet somehow miraculously made millions in office—before exiting through a gold-plated revolving door to Wall Street, Silicon Valley, or a K Street lobbying shop.

A word about President Donald Trump. He is his own worst enemy. If he doesn't stop using "alternative facts" and criticizing anyone who doesn't agree with him, he may not have a second term. His favorite words are "believe me," but he has a hard time trying to find what the word "truth" is. It has been shown that President Trump is a compulsive liar. The sad and dangerous part is that he doesn't know when he is lying. He always believes he is telling the truth and he never knows when he is wrong. Trump has the biggest ego of anyone I know or have ever heard of. Another self-appreciating word he uses more than any other president has ever used is the word "me." Obama comes in second.

In a letter to the editor of *The Economist* on July 20, 2017 titled "Why Trump Succeeds," Professor Mark Wolfgram, Visiting Fellow, Carleton University, Ottawa, wrote

Regarding your special report on Donald Trump's America (July 1st), in "Strangers in Their Own Land," Arlie Russell Hochschild provides a metaphorical story as an insight into the roots of American populism. The American Dream is just over the hill and everyone is in line, but the line is moving slower than it used to. At the very point the line begins to slow, women, blacks, and other minorities begin to cut in line. Not only that, but the federal government helps them cut in line. When those already in line complain, they are called rednecks, white trash, and Bible thumpers. They become angry.

Affirmative action is hugely unpopular with white voters. Cutting in line violates a fundamental sense of justice. Republicans have run against affirmative action for decades and yet done very little to change the policies. Then Mr. Trump arrives and berates mainstream Republicans, humiliating them in the debates, which become something akin to a professional wrestling match. The backlash against affirmative action is gathering strength and clarity. This is the result of telling white Americans that identity politics is an issue of justice, just not for them.

Today's Democratic Party is a little too far left, almost socialistic. I think Margaret Thatcher said it best: "Socialism is a great form of government until the other people run out of money."

As you read this book, you might wonder why I went from a fifty-year Democrat to an eight-year Republican, and for now, an unaffiliated voter. Today, according to the North Carolina Board of Elections website, there are 2,640,713 Democratic voters, 2,054,832 Republican voters, and 2,043,809 unaffiliated voters in North Carolina. In large urban counties, such as Wake and Mecklenburg, unaffiliated voters already exceed Republicans by a wide margin. The unaffiliated voter seems to be the trend today as more folks are abandoning both traditional parties because of their control by strident extremes.

The Democratic Party over the years did a lot of great things, and I enjoyed being a part of it. As so many like me have said, the Democratic Party left me, I didn't leave them. A white male businessman has little place in the Democratic Party today. In 2002 I started working for a few Republicans, who I think did a lot of good things, but eventually they were also taken over by the extremes. Neither the Democrats nor the Republicans can win an election today without the unaffiliated vote, and the unaffiliated vote will soon be the majority voters. Hopefully something good will happen.

Credits and Acknowledgments

DESIGN AND ILLUSTRATIONS

Jerry Miller. One of Cary's most renowned artists, Jerry did all the illustrations and worked tirelessly with me on the inspiration for the design of the book and its cover. Jerry has done over a thousand illustrations of buildings in North Carolina.

WRITING AND EDITING

Carolyn Rawls Booth. Carolyn is a local writer who has published three books of historical fiction and several regional cookbooks. Carolyn is a friend and neighbor who generously offered her editing and writing skills to help me with this book.

W. C. (Bill) Jones Jr. Bill is a longtime friend and my business partner. He spent many hours reviewing, adding text, editing, typing, and correcting my mistakes.

Jackson Freeman. Jackson is a longtime resident of Raleigh and a recent graduate of the University of North Carolina. He assisted in the formatting and editing of this book.

Thomas W. Bradshaw Jr. I have known Tom about sixty years, and we have worked on many political campaigns and on many charitable organizations together. His contributions to this little book have been most helpful. Tom was mayor of Raleigh, mayor of Bald Head Island, and Head of the Department of Transportation under Governor Jim

Hunt. While he was in office, he started the planning of the I-40 corridor from Raleigh to Wilmington. Tom could have written this book a whole lot better than me, but at the age of seventy-eight he is still going full-time trying to help raise $50 million for a charitable organization. He has done much for North Carolina and still does.

Charles Heatherly. Charles was in my National Guard unit, and we worked together on many campaigns. He was the director of the North Carolina Division of Travel and Tourism, and served with the late state treasurer, Harlan Bowles, as one of his deputies.

A WORD ABOUT MY FAMILY

Most families today are scattered across the country, and mine is no different. None of them live in or near me in Cary, North Carolina. I have lived in Cary over sixty years and I don't ever plan on leaving. My children and grandchildren are one of the most important parts of my life. One of my daughters, Melanie, lives in Lebanon, Ohio, with her husband Tom. They have two sons, Stuart and Lee— good 'ole southern names. Stuart is in the ninth grade and is not only smart, but a good athlete and will probably play for the New York Yankees someday. Lee is in his second year at the University of Kentucky studying on an engineering scholarship and is extremely smart. Melanie is a full-time housewife and a perfect mother. Tom is a dedicated father who is very involved in his sons' activities. My other daughter, Michele, is a very accomplished executive and is currently director of finance at the Hudson Institute in Washington, DC. My son Ray Jr. passed away June 18, 2015. He was fifty-eight years old and I can describe him in one sentence: *If God had let me design my own son, I can't think of one thing I would have changed about him.* He and his wife Mary had four children: two sons, Raymond and William, who are college graduates and very successful young men, and two daughters, Kerry and Christine, who are also college graduates and both very gifted. Mary is a lawyer and is one of the sweetest and toughest people you will ever want to meet. Even though I am surely impossible to deal with, she somehow keeps me in line.

My grandson Raymond (Ray Jr.'s son) and his beautiful wife Lara just had a baby girl named Caroline, who is my first great-grandchild. She is one of the smartest, most beautiful great-granddaughters I have ever seen. Of course, all of my children, grandchildren, and great-grandchildren take after me. There are no snowflakes in my family.

Melba's side of the family has been great to me. Her sister Shirley and Shirley's husband Ron and all her family try to look after me. They are the only family members who live in this area. Shirley calls me almost every day, and I know I can always count on her and her family.

My wife Melba was one of the most beautiful people, both inside and out, that I have ever met. She and my son passed away from cancer in the past two years. Some days I get a little lonely and down and out, but with a family like mine, it is hard to feel too bad.

Thank God for Facebook. When I am feeling a little down, all I have to do is open Facebook and look at my great-granddaughter Caroline, and she cheers me up for several days. I must have a hundred pictures of her.

Caroline Ebert

References

Cline, Ned. *The Walter Davis Story: One Man Who Made a Difference.* n.p.: Ned Cline, 2009.

Christensen, Rob. *The Paradox of Tar Heel Politics: The Personalities, Elections, and Events that Shaped Modern North Carolina.* Chapel Hill: University of North Carolina Press, 2008.

Jeffreys, Grady and Charles Heatherly. *Jim Gardner: A Question of Character.* Raleigh: Patriot Press, 1992.

Powell, William S., ed. *Encyclopedia of North Carolina.* Chapel Hill: University of North Carolina Press, 2006.